MW01196028

--The--
Rachel Plummer
Narrative

A stirring narrative of adventure, hardship and privation in the early days of Texas, depicting struggles with the Indians and other adventures.

Picture of Quanna Parker, Chief of Comanche Indians,
now deceased.

Foreword

In presenting this little book to the public, our aim and desire is to impress or refresh the minds of the people of the hardships and suffering the pioneer settlers of Texas had to endure in opening the way for the blessings and civilization the people of Texas now enjoy. We realize the fact, that half has never yet been told, no doubt it never will all be told. Our grandfather has only given a brief sketch of his travels and trials while seeking to rescue his daughter and grandson from captivity by the Redmen; also his niece, Cyntha Ann Parker, that was captured at the Parker Fort massacre on the Navasota River; and it is not our desire to rekindle the *ill* feelings between the Redmen and the Paleface men, that existed between the two tribes at that time. We would much rather strengthen, amity confidence and good will between the tribes.

Who knows what suffering and grief those people endured with the captivity of the little girl, Cyntha Ann Parker, who in later years became the wife of a favorite Comanche Chief. Then in the due course of time became the *mother* of the noted Chief Quanna Parker, who in later years, by his great influence over the Redmen, persuaded and prevented the Redmen from wageing a cruel war on the Paleface. On one occasion the Redmen declared war on the Paleface; Quanna alone opposed the war and they held another council and because of the Paleface blood in his veins they declared him a traitor to the Redmen, and condemned him to be put to death. He told them, "the Paleface have many braves; we have only a few braves; our braves will all be killed by the many Paleface braves; save our braves, raise more braves, and become a great nation like the Paleface." *Yet* they declared he must die. "I am willing to die for my braves, give me a fair chance; fight me singly, one at a time; do not take advantage and double on me, and I will fight you to the death to save my braves." In this one act, he no doubt averted war and preserved many lives of both tribes, as well as much suffering and distress. Is it the *unseen* hand of providence? Who knows, who can say, of a truth, it is, or is not.

In offering this little narrative to the public, we are sorry the first 10 pages are incomplete, having been torn and destroyed. Hoping the public will give this little narrative a liberal

3

patronage and careful consideration, of its contents, and think if we of today do not owe to the memory of all of the pioneers who blazed the way in this great State, for our present enjoyment and blessings; we say all, not only those mentioned in this little book, but all who helped in the struggle in those perilous times, a gratitude of which language is not at our command to express.

Respectfully,

MRS. JANE KENNEDY, Granddaughter of
    J. W. Parker.
MRS. RACHEL LOFTON, Greatgranddaughter.
MRS. SUSIE HENDRIX, Granddaughter.

CHAPTER II.

Capture of Fort Parker—inhuman butchery of its inmates— Marvelous escape of my brother's wife and two children— Mrs. Duty, my mother-in-law, stabbed by the Indians and left as dead—sufferings of my family and those with us in escaping to the Settlement—order of troops to our relief and their recall to meet the Mexicans—the scene at the fort on my return with fourteen men.

On the 19th day of May, 1836, Parker's Fort, under my command, was captured by a band of the Comanche and other tribes of Indians, under the following circumstances. A few days previous to the day above named, I had disbanded the troops under my command, as there appeared to be but little danger of an attack, and the Government was not in a condition to bear the expense of supporting troops, unless the circumstances were of such a nature as to imperiously demand it. On the morning of the day before mentioned, myself, two of my sons-in-law, and my oldest son, had repaired to the farm, a short distance from the fort, to finish laying by our crop of corn; leaving in the fort, my father, (Elder John Parker,) my two brothers, Benjamin and Silas, and family, my wife and six children, including Mrs. Plummer, whose narrative is annexed to this book, Mrs. Nixon, my mother-in-law, Mrs. Duty, Mr. Frost and family, my sister-in-law, Mrs. Kellogg, Mr. Dwight and his family; making in all thirty-four, eighteen of whom were children. About an hour after I left the fort, a band of Indians approached it, bearing a *white flag;* and when my brother Benjamin went out to meet them, he was told their object was peace, and that they had come to make a treaty with the whites. This treacherous *ruse* was too successful. It threw those in the fort so much off their guard that it was not until the enemy had almost entirely surrounded them and had manifested their hostile intentions by killing my brother Benjamin, who was in their hands, that any attempt was made either to resist or escape.*

Before this, however, my daughter, Mrs. Nixon, becoming alarmed, had left the fort, and ran to the field to alarm us. Before she reached us we heard her screams, and ran immediately

---

* The reader is referred to the appended narrative of Rachel Plummer, for particulars of what then occurred.

to meet her. She, in most breathless anxiety, informed us of what was going on at the fort, and we all immediately started for the fort. We had not proceeded more than a few hundred yards before we met my wife and children, who confirmed what my daughter had told us. It was immediately agreed upon by us that I should take my wife and children to a place of concealment, that Mr. Plummer should proceed to alarm some neighbors about half a mile off, and that Mr. Nixon should go on to the fort. I proceeded to place my family in a place of safety, which I did by directing my course to the river Navisott, about half a mile distant, which I succeeded in crossing with my wife and children. Having placed them where I thought they would be safe, I retraced my steps for the purpose of reaching the fort as soon as possible. On re-crossing the river, I met Mrs. Frost and her family, in the care of Mr. Dwight, who had also escaped from the fort, and Mr. Dwight informed me that he had been overtaken by Mr. Nixon, who informed him that he had been to the fort, and that all was lost; either killed or taken prisoners! As Mr. Nixon approached the fort, he discovered a company of Indians who were dragging off my brother Silas' wife and children, four in number, as prisoners. With a bravery scarcely paralleled in any warfare, he drew his gun to his shoulder and rushed upon the enemy, some forty or fifty in number, and although he did not fire, (which under the circumstances would have been not only useless but very hazardous,) succeeded by his daring boldness and determined appearance, in effecting the rescue of the mother and two of her children; while the Indians succeeded in carrying off the other two children, one of whom is yet a prisoner among them, and whose release I hope, in the Providence of God, to be able to effect, by the means this humble narrative may place in my hands.

My father, mother-in-law, and Mrs. Kellogg, my sister-in-law, made their escape from the fort, and had proceeded about three-fourths of a mile, when they were overtaken by the enemy and stripped of their clothing, and the two first named were murdered—my father being shot through with an arrow, and scalped—my mother-in-law being stabbed with a knife, and left as dead; while my sister-in-law, Mrs. Kellogg, was taken off as a prisoner. Mr. Frost and his son Robert were slain in the fort, from whence was taken Mrs. Plummer and her child, about 18 months old, as prisoners. Thus were five slain, one badly

6

wounded, and five taken prisoners, and twenty-three made their escape.

Mr. Plummer having succeeded in alarming the neighbors, he, in company with some fifteen others, returned to the fort just as the Indians, after having stripped it of every thing, destroyed the cattle, and secured the horses, were leaving it. The Indians being seven or eight hundred strong, they did not attack or attempt to follow them; but retreated to the woods, where they concealed themselves until the next day, when they proceeded to another settlement about sixty miles east of the fort, near Fort Houston.

Mr. Nixon, after having gallantly released the prisoners, as mentioned, and having placed them in the care of Mr. Plummer and his company, turned his attention to myself and those with me. In passing through the river bottom, we often came to sandy places where we could be tracked. If there was necessity for flight, I thougnt there was also necessity for precaution, and accordingly when I came to those sandy places, I made all the company pass over them by walking backwards, in order that our tracks would present the appearance of our having gone in a contrary direction from the one we were pursuing, and thus deceive the Indians, should they attempt to follow our trail. This *ruse* deceived Mr. Nixon, who after a fruitless search of two days to find us, gave us up, supposing that we also had fallen into the hands of the savages. Whilst he was thus wandering about, undetermined what to do, he accidentally found Mrs. Duty, who had been stabbed in the right breast with a large knife, which did not enter the chest, but passed off near her ribs. He was passing near her after dark and heard her groans, and on approaching her, found her in a dying and most pitiable condition. It had been twelve or fourteen hours since she was stabbed, and faint with the loss of blood, stripped of every vestige of clothing, she lay mangled and bleeding on the cold ground, in a dark and howling wilderness, while her life-blood was fast ebbing from her wound. He at first attempted to remove her, but she fainted in his arms; and his only means of reviving her, was by bringing water to her in his shoe. This he repeated several times, and finally, after great exertion, succeeded in getting her to a neighboring house, though it was deserted. Before the morning, he succeeded in finding the company raised by Mr. Plummer, when all the attention was rendered her their situation afforded, and her wounds dressed. She was taken along by the company that went to the settlement near Fort Houston, where she recovered, but has subsequently died.

Mr. Plummer, in searching for his wife and child, was separated from this company, and wandered through the country, and finally made his way to Tinning's settlement, on the Navasott, which he reached soon after my arrival there.

I must, however, ask the reader to go back and accompany myself, my family, Mrs. Frost and her family, and Mr. Dwight and his family, making in all 18 persons, from the time we crossed the Navasott, near Fort Parker, until we reached this settlement, a distance of 90 miles, the way we were compelled to travel it.

I must leave it to the mind of the reader to conjecture, if it can, for it is beyond the ability of my pen to describe the feelings that filled the breasts of myself and my almost helpless companions in sorrow and suffering. There we were in the howling wilderness, barefooted and bareheaded—a savage and relentless foe on the one hand; on the other, a trackless and uninhabited country literally covered with venomous reptiles and ravenous beasts—destitute of one mouthful of food, and the means of procuring it—our fathers, mothers, and children, having all, except those composing our company, just fallen a prey, as we supposed, to savage barbarity; and fearfully expecting at every step to share their fate ourselves—all, all rushed upon our minds like a blighting sirocco—it made the soul sick—despair seized upon the heart, and reason well-nigh deserted her throne.

I have stated that our company consisted of 18 persons. Of this number, 12 were children from 1 to 12 years of age. I desired, after night had come on, to return to the fort, to see if I could procure some food and information of what had become of those who were with us—whether they were slain, or had made their escape—but my companions said they would rather risk starving than I should leave them, fearing I would fall into the hands of the enemy, in which event, they knew they would perish in the wilderness, as they were all alike ignorant of the course to pursue to reach a settlement, and of the proper precaution to avoid falling into the hands of the enemy. I therefore determined to start for the settlement.

As it was prudent that we should travel at night and remain concealed in the day, I directed the women and children to conceal themselves in the briars, and I climbed a tall tree, by which I was enabled to recnnoitre the fort. All was silent as death.

8

I in vain strained my eyes to see some living object, and listened to hear some human voice about the fort. Descending from the tree, I took one of my children on my shoulder, and led another; the other grown persons followed my example, and we started through the thickly entangled briars and underbush in the direction of the settlement. My wife was in very delicate health. Mrs. Frost's grief at the loss of her husband and son was inconsolable; and all being barefooted, except my wife and Mrs. Frost, our progress was very slow. Many of the children had nothing on but a shirt; and their sufferings from the briars tearing their flesh and wounding their feet, was almost beyond endurance.

We traveled until about three o'clock in the morning, when the women and children being worn out by fatigue and hunger, we lay down upon the grass and slept until the dawn of day, when we again resumed our weary journey. Here we left the river bottom, in order to avoid the briars; but from the many tracks of Indians and horses on the high lands, it was evident that the Indians were hunting us; and like the fox in the fable, we were again compelled to take to the river bottom; for though the brambles did indeed tear our flesh, yet they preserved our lives from danger. Repeatedly, yes, in some places, every few steps, did I see the briars tear the legs of the little children until the blood trickled down so that they could have been tracked by it.

It was now the night of the second day, and all, especially the children and the women giving suck, began to suffer intensely with hunger. We were now immediately on the bank of the river, and through the mercy of Providence, a skunk (or polecat,) came in our way. I immediately pursued it, and after much trouble, I succeeded in catching it as it jumped into the river; and the only way I could kill it, was by holding it under the water until it was drowned. Having fortunately brought with us the means for striking fire, we soon had it cooked and equally divided amongst our company; and the portion to each was small, indeed. This was all we had to eat until the fourth day in the evening, when we were so fortunate as to capture another skunk and two small terrapins, which were also cooked and divided.

The fifth day, in the evening, I found that the women and children were too much exhausted from hunger and fatigue, and their feet so sore, that it was impossible for them to travel any farther. After holding a consultation, it was agreed upon that I should go on to the settlement, it being now about 35 miles distant, and that Mr. Wright should remain with the company. Accordingly, the next morning, I started for the settlement, which I reached early in the afternoon.

I have often looked back and been astonished at this extraordinary feat. In the last six days I had not eaten one mouthful of food, (for while the others had partaken of the animals before mentioned, I had given my share to the children,) and yet I walked thirty-five miles in about eight hours. But the thought of the unfortunate sufferers I had left behind instilled in me that strength and perseverance known only to those who may have been placed in a similar situation. God, in his bountiful mercy, strengthened and upheld me in this trying hour of need, and to Him do I most humbly give all the praise and glory.

The first house I met with was Capt. Carter's, who received me kindly, and promptly offered me all the aid in his power. He soon had five horses prepared, and himself and Jeremiah Courtney accompanied me to meet our little company of sufferers. Just at dark, we met them, and placing the women and children upon the horses, we arrived at Capt. Carter's about midnight. Here we received all that kind attention and relief which our wretched condition demanded, and that benevolent and sympathetic hearts could bestow.

We arrived at Capt. Carter's on the 25th of May. On the following day, my son-in-law, Mr. Plummer, arrived there also; he having given us up as lost, and started for the same settlement at which we arrived.

On the 27th, I started an express to the officers of the Government for assistance. Maj. John W. Moody bore the express, and five hundred troops were promptly ordered to our relief. These troops had proceeded as far as Washington, when they received the intelligence that the defeated army of Santa Anna was returning upon the western frontier,* and they were ordered to meet them. Thus was my design of returning immediately to the fort, and of pursuing the Indians and releasing the prisoners, frustrated. To go alone was useless, and to raise a company was impossible, as every person capable of serving was already in the Texas army.

By this time, my other son-in-law, Nixon, having arrived safely at the settlement of Fort Houston, about 150 miles distant

---

* This, however, turned out to be untrue.

10

from where we were, whither he had conducted those who had made their escape, among whom was Mrs. Duty, who was now fast recovering from her wound. Hearing that we had arrived at Capt. Carter's, he came to us; and from him we learned the particulars, as to the number killed and taken prisoners. This was the first certain intelligence Mrs. Frost had of the death of her husband and son.

Thinking that my family would not be entirely safe from the Indians in a situation so far out on the frontier as the residence of Capt. Carter, I removed them farther back into the interior, in Grimes' Settlement.* Here I procured a house, or, rather, a part of one, for there was another family living in it. The house was small, and had nothing but a dirt floor. I was entirely without money, or any means of procuring the necessities, much less, the comforts of life. Nor were they to be procured if I had the means, for they were not in that section of the country, so, making a virtue of necessity, I made the best arrangements I was able for the comfort of my family, preparatory to returning to the fort. I made a kind of scaffold in one corner of the cabin by driving four forks into the ground, across which, I laid some slab boards; upon these boards, was laid some straw, which was to serve as a bed.

Just as I had completed my arrangement for starting back to the fort, all of my family were taken sick with the measles; but, leaving them to the charity of the neighbors and to the mercy of Providence, I set off, accompanied by thirteen others. On our arrival at the fort, on the 19th of June—exactly one month from the time we left—we found the houses still standing, but the crops were entirely destroyed, the horses stolen, nearly all the cattle killed, and not a single article of household furniture left.

We remained at the fort three days; during which time, I was enabled to gather the bones of my father and two brothers, and those of Mr. Frost and his son; their flesh having been devoured by wild beasts.

We made a rough box, into which we deposited their remains, (except those of my youngest brother, which I preserved, as he and I had entered into an agreement, that whichever survived, should see that his brother's body was not buried,) and having dug a grave, they were buried. As I assisted in perform-

* To the Hon. Judge Grimes, A. Montgomery, and others, I shall ever feel grateful for their kindness to my distressed family.

ing this last sad service to their remains, I, in the bitter anguish of my soul, exclaimed, "rest my father and rest my brothers— rest—would to God I were with you."

Finding that we could make no discoveries as to the route the Indians had taken with the prisoners, we determined to return to the settlement; so gathering as many of our cattle as we could find, we started back. On my arrival in the neighborhood of my family, I met Dr. Adams, who was attending my wife. He informed me that my wife, as he thought, must die. As if it were revealed from heaven, I felt she would not die; and so I told the doctor, asking him, at the same time, the privilege of using his medicines, which he freely granted. I was confident that my wife's disease was as much of the mind as of the body, and directed my course accordingly. On my coming in the presence of my wife, I was horror-stricken. There she lay on a pallet of straw literally reduced to skin and bones; she was entirely bereft of reason, and appeared to have lost all sense of pain. Oh God! how my soul was pierced when she gazed upon me with her ghastly eyes! By her side lay my youngest child, having more the appearance of a corpse than a living being. Breathing a prayer to God for his merciful intercession, I applied the medicines as my best judgment dictated, and after seven days of unceasing watching and painful suspense, I was made to rejoice, through the mercy of God, in beholding my wife again restored to reason, and evidently convalescent. She finally recovered, as also did my child.

CHAPTER III.

My removal to my present residence—my visits to Gen. Houston and other influential gentlemen, to endeavor to create feelings so far in my behalf, as to afford me some help in effecting the release of the prisoners—my sister-in-law, Mrs. Kellogg, purchased by some Delaware Indians and brough in—a condensed account of several trips made myself and others through the Indian nations, seeking the prisoners.

Soon after the recovery of my family, I removed to Jessy Parker's, about 50 miles distant. And here I must express the grateful feelings I shall ever entertain for the kindnesses extended to myself and family by this most generous hearted man, who though of the same name, but no way related to me, yet the many favors he bestowed on us, proved his whole-souled generosity and Christian feeling. In the neighborhood of Mr. Parker I purchased a tract of land of Benson Risinghoover, upon which I built me a temporary camp; and having fixed my family as comfortably as I could, on the 11th of July I started to see Gen. Houston.

All I desired, was, that he should grant me a company of men. On my arrival at Col. Sublett's, near San Augustine, where Gen. Houston was confined at the time, from the wound he received at the battle of San Jacinto; and having laid my plans before him for retaking the prisoners, he decided against it, and insisted that a treaty with the Indians would be the most effective and expeditious means of releasing the prisoners. I contended that such a thing as a treaty being formed with hostile Indians until they were whipped, and well whipped, had never been known; and the more thorough the chastisement, the more lasting the treaty. All argument failed, however, and with a heavy heart and perplexed mind, I retraced my steps to the humble abode of my afflicted family. I then thought that Gen. Houston betrayed too great an indifference to the matter; though this impression, no doubt, grew out of the great anxiety felt on my part.

I arrived at home on the 12th of August, and on the 13th, I went to see Col. Nathaniel Robbins, to enlist his influence in our behalf. He accompanied me to Nacogdoches, whence

, 13

Gen. Houston had gone; and we again endeavored to persuade him to order an expedition against the Comanches; but with no success.

Feeling that Gen. Houston might think that we were seeking the glory of the expedition, which would, if gotten up, be among his divisions, we informed him that we did not desire the honors, but preferred taking our stations in the ranks. The general, however, was inexorable, and still insisted upon the advisability of a treaty.

Col. Robbins, as much chagrined at our want of success as myself, returned home—and here I must remark of this good man, who now sleeps with his fathers, that for nobleness of soul, true philanthropy, and high-toned gentlemanly deportment, his equal were few, and superiors he had none.

I then determined to visit Col. Richard Sparks, with the plan in view, that had induced me to call on Col. Robbins; however, it did no good, and I returned again to Nacogdoches, where I arrived on the 20th of August. Here I was rejoiced to meet with my sister-in-law, Mrs. Kellogg, who had been purchased by some Delaware Indians, and brought in. The consideration claimed by the Indians for their services, was $150, which Gen. Houston generously paid, as I was penniless.

I immediately started, with Mrs. Kellogg, accompanied by Mr. Milligan and several other gentlemen, for home, a distance of 140 miles. On the 22nd, we fell in with a Mr. Smith, who had just discovered two Indians stealing horses. He had shot one a few hundred yards from the road, and we turned off to see the dead Indian. On reaching the spot where he lay, we found that Mr. Smith had partially missed his aim, for the ball had merely grazed his forehead. Mrs. Kellogg immediately recognized the Indian, as not only being one of the band that had captured Fort Parker, but the very one that had shot and scalped my father; in confirmation of which, she said, if he was the same, he had a scar on each arm, as if cut with a knife. I immediately examined him, and found, with mingled feelings of joy, sorrow, and revenge, the scars as described:—joy at the opportunity of avenging the butchery of my father, and sorrow at the recollection of it. The Indian hearing a familiar female voice, raised his head, and gazing with looks of surprise and doubt upon Mrs. Kellogg, he at length appeared to recognize her, and muttering something I did not understand, fell back, pretending to be dead. He had left her a prisoner in his town, when he

14

and several others of his tribe started on this trip of murder and plunder—hence, his marked surprise on seeing her at liberty and with her friends. What followed, it is unnecessary to relate—suffice it to say, that it was the unanimous verdict of the company, that he would never kill and scalp another white man.

On the 6th of September, we arrived at home, joyous was the meeting of my wife and her sister. Mrs. Kellogg could give us no intelligence of any of the other prisoners, as the party of Indians that captured the Fort, dispersed in a few days after —the Ketchaws taking her, one tribe of the Comanches taking my daughter and her child, and another tribe of the same nation, taking my nephew and niece, the children of my brother Silas.

After much consideration and consultation with my friends as to the best course to pursue, I determined to go to Coffee's trading house on Red River, about 700 miles distant, to see if I could hear any thing of the prisoners, or make any arrangements to have them purchased and brought in.

Accordingly, on the 15th of September, I started, and on the 27th, arrived at Jonesborough, on Red River, where I was treated with much kindness by Maj L. W. Tinnin, Col. John Fowler, and many others. The gentlemen named, offered to loan me money; but as I had no use for money where I was going, I declined accepting it. To Mr. Johnson, of that place, I am indebted for many kindnesses, for which I offered him a remuneration, but he would not accept it. My horse having given out, I left him at Mr. Johnson's, of whom I purchased another, and proceeded on to Coffee's establishment.

On the 2nd day of October, I heard that a woman had been brought in to Capt. Pace's, on Blue River, who I thought, from the description, was my daughter. I immediately determined to go to Pace's, distant about 80 miles, the way I was compelled to travel. Not being able to get my horse across Red River, I left him with Mr. Fitzgerald, with directions, that should I not return to his house within ten days, he should let my family know that I was dead, as I had determined to return within that time, if alive. Having, with the assistance of Mr. Stewart, made a raft, I crossed Red River. I could obtain no reliable information as to the course I should pursue, and there being no road, or even trace, I directed my course according to the best information I could obtain. Mrs. Fitzgerald had furnished me with some meat and bread, which I lost before I had gone far, as

I had great difficulty in passing through the swamps and thickets of the river bottom. I had prepared myself with a pocket compass by which I was enabled to direct my course. I walked as far as I could the first day, and at night found myself on a prairie. Being much fatigued I lay down upon the grass to sleep—but the thought that I was so near my child, it drove sleep from my eyes. I would sometimes doze for a few moments, but would soon arouse with an effort to embrace the object of my care and pursuit. I would have travelled all night, but I could not see the points of my compass, and the night being cloudy, I could not have kept my course.

The next morning, I started as soon as it was light enough to see my compass, and notwithstanding my feet were blistered and I had recovered but little from my fatigue of the previous day, I must have traveled forty miles before dark. At night, being yet on this prairie, and the ground being wet, I found it would be impossible to sleep without fire; so having found a few scrubby saplings, I broke off some brush and kindled a fire. It now commenced thundering and threatened a storm, which soon came on. The rain fell in torrents whilst the almost unceasing flashes of lightning and deafening thunder, made me feel, in my lonely condition, as if "the war of elements, the wreck of matter, and the crush of worlds," was about to be consummated.

By the flashes of lightning, I could see far around me, and the prairie presented the appearance of one unbroken sheet of water. Where I stood, the water was at least two feet deep. I had two small pistols, which I kept dry by wrapping my shirt around them and placing one under each arm. To this timely precaution, I undoubtedly owe the preservation of my life. About two o'clock in the morning, the wind changed to the North, and in less than one hour my clothes were frozen upon me, and I felt that I could not live until morning. Though unable to direct my course in the dark, I was compelled to keep in motion, or freeze to death, so I promenaded a space of forty or fifty yards, in the water a foot deep, until morning. During this time the snow fell fast, but melted as it fell.

As soon as it was light I pursued my journey, with little hope of being alive at night, or ever again beholding the face of a human being. About 9 o'clock, I saw a body of timber to the Southeast, whither I directed my steps. My progress was very slow and difficult, as the grass being about two feet high, was matted together by the ice. On reaching the woods, I seated my-

16

self upon a log to rest. I had sat there but a few minutes when I found it very difficult to keep from going to sleep. This was produced by the extreme cold; my feet and hands had lost all sense of pain, and I knew I was fast freezing to death. I attempted to rise, but could not. There was a small tree within my reach, and taking hold of it I succeeded in rising to my feet. In the short time I had been still, my limbs had become so stiffened, that I could not walk. I was afraid to let go the tree, for fear I should fall, in which case I knew I should never rise.

It is impossible for the mind to form any just conception of my feelings at this time. I have often attempted to call to mind how I felt, but in vain; it appears like a dream, and often, when reflecting on the event, I almost doubt its reality.

To remain stationary was certain death—so there was but one alternative left—move I must. There was an old dry log about fifty yards from me, and my life depended on my being able to reach it and strike a fire. Letting go the tree I ventured on this hazardous experiment, and moving my feet but a few inches at first, I succeeded, after much exertion of nearly an hour, in gaining the log. Having cut some dry pieces of cotton from my shirt, and loaded one of my pistols with them, I discharged it against a dry part of the log. My agonizing fears and suspense were soon relieved by the success of this effort to start a fire, and soon my frozen clothing began to yield to the influence of the heat, and it was not long before my sense of pain returned.

The pain I had suffered from cold, during the last twelve hours, was, I thought, as great as the human system could endure; but it was comparatively nothing to that I felt in getting warm. Had my hands and feet been held in the fire until consumed, the pain certainly could not have been greater. When entirely restored to a proper warmth, my hands and feet stung and smarted as if they had been burned, and the skin peeled off them.

Three days had now elapsed since I had tasted food, and it required the exercise of all the fortitude and courage I was master of to keep me from sinking down with fatigue and hunger. The hope of soon seeing my lost child, added a new vigor to my body, and summoning all my remaining strength I pursued my journey.

I had not proceeded far, before night came on, and having made a good fire, I sunk down upon the cold, damp ground, to rest. My fatigue acted as an opiate, and I soon yielded myself to the arms of Morpheus, with but little hopes of ever again awaking in this world. I slept soundly all night; and although my fire had gone out, and my clothes were frozen to the ground, my hair a mat of ice, and my limbs benumbed, God, in His merciful preservation, enabled me to rise and rekindle the fire. After my clothes were thawed and partially dried, my limbs again became controllable, and I pursued my journey. I could not tell whether I had passed Mr. Pace's or not; but to attempt to return to the settlement I had left, would be vain; so, exercising my best judgment, I directed my course, with scarcely a hope of surviving until night. I suppose I traveled that day about fifteen miles. The sun was now setting, and I almost hoped I would not live to see it rise. Darkness came on apace; and oh, how horrible was the thought of having to spend another night in the wild wilderness, eight hundred miles from home, with the frozen ground for a bed, and the blue dome of heaven my only shelter. As these thoughts were revolving in my mind, I heard a calf bleat—and the songs of angels could not have been sweeter to my ear, or more charming to my soul, than was the bleat of that calf. With an energy that astonished me, I pushed on in the direction from whence the sound came; and just at dark a grateful heart to God for his wonderful mercies, I found myself seated in Pace's house, by a comfortable fire; while his kind wife was preparing me a cup of coffee.

My joy at the escape I had made from a miserable death in the wilderness, was, however, soon turned to mortification and sorrow, for I learned that the woman that had been brought in was not my daughter, but a Mrs. Yorkins. She had gone on to Samuel B. Marshall's, and I did not get to see her.

At Pace's however, I met with some of Coffee's traders, who gave me direct intelligence of my daughter. They informed me that she was in charge of a band of Indians, who, they said, were then encamped about 60 miles from Mr. Pace's. They also informed me that the Indians had killed my daughter's child. The intelligence kindled anew the flame that was raging in my breast; and I immediately determined to go to the camp of the Indians, and at the risk of my life, recover my daughter.

I remained at Pace's two nights and one day, during which time, I received all the attention and kindness he and his family could bestow, for which I shall ever feel grateful.

On the morning of my departure from Mr. Pace's, his kind lady prepared me some bread and venison to take with me, though it was not more than enough to last one day. In very little better condition than when I arrived at Mr. Pace's, I directed my course to the Indian camp, which I did not reach until the fourth day in the afternoon. The Indians, I found, had left there just after the heavy rain before spoken of. As I could now follow them by their trail, I started on, and on the 6th day, I arrived at Red River. The Indians had crossed the river, and as I knew that in my enfeebled condition I could not swim it, and there being no timber near with which I could make a raft, I was compelled to retrace my steps.

On turning homeward and contemplating my situation, I felt as certain as that I was then alive, that I should never again see home. Faint with hunger and fatigue, and all hopes of ever again seeing my unfortunate daughter, being, as I thought, cut off, I resigned myself to my fate. I looked down the river and saw some timber, and feeling that I would rather die among the trees than in an open prairie, thither I directed my steps; and just as the sun was setting, I reached the spot which I never expected to leave. I pray God that when the final hour does come, and He shall call me hence, that I may feel as willing to obey as I did then.

I had been seated on a log in these woods but a few minutes, when I heard a rustling in the leaves; and on looking round, I saw a skunk near me; and at the same moment I saw it, I felt that the kind protecting care of Providence was yet around, and I was firmly convinced in my mind that I should again see my family, as I had been a few moments before persuaded that I should not.

Inscrutable, indeed, are the ways of Providence! Often, when we have the least occasion to fear death, we are stricken down without a moment's warning; whilst, on the other hand, when we have no reason to hope for life, and sincerely pray for death, the hand of the all-wise and merciful God is stretched forth, and we are plucked from the cold embrace of the "King of Terrors," as a "brand from the burning!"

I speedily despatched the skunk, and soon had a part of it broiling on the fire; and though I ate but a small portion that night, it strengthened and revived me so much, that the next morning I set about making a raft. This was the first food I had tasted in the last six days.

The reader doubtless thinks it strange that I had not a gun with me on such a tour. I neglected to mention, that when I

19

arrived at Mr. Tinnie's, soon after I had started on this journey, he proposed to go and engage some Shawnee Indians to go in search of the prisoners, and required the loan of my gun. I let him have it, and he did not return before I left, so I went on without it.

Having burned some logs that lay near the river, into several pieces, I soon tied them together with bark and grape vines. Upon this raft I descended Red River, to Mr. Fitzgerald's, where I arrived on the 22nd, after an absence of twenty days. Mr. Fitzgerald had not written to my family, as I directed, not having met with an opportunity of sending the letter.

Considering all efforts to regain my daughter, fruitless, my duty to my family required my immediate return home, which I reached on the 17th day of November.

Congress being now in session, at Columbia, I determined to go there and petition that body for some assistance. But a treaty was urged as the best and only means of effecting the release of the prisoners, and I was doomed again to return home in sorrowful hopelessness.

Having firmly determined never to cease my efforts to facilitate the release of the prisoners, I concluded to visit Gen. T. J. Rusk and Maj. J. W. Burton, and try to enlist them in my cause. I found them both willing to render me all the assistance in their power; but they could do nothing. I again went to see Col. R. Sparks, but to no effect.

I now determined to return to Red River, and see what could be done; and taking leave of my family on the 25th day of February, 1837, I started on this, my second tour, among the Indians. I arrived at Natchitoches on the 7th of March, where I received many kindnesses from Mr. Joseph S. March, Mr. Clark, near Spanish Town, and others. Here I offered a reward of $300 for every prisoner then among the Indians that might be brought in; and to Mr. D. P. Despelier, I am under obligations for the gratuitous insertion of the advertisement in his paper.

On the 10th, I left Natchitoches for Monroe, to endeavor to collect some money due me, in order to pay the offered rewards, if needed. The waters being very high, and having many streams to cross, my progress was very slow and disagreeable, which was greatly increased by an unceasing toothache, with which I suffered nearly the whole way. On the 19th, I lost my pocket-book, and had to return a distance of twenty miles before I found it. I arrived at Monroe on the 20th, where I succeeded in collecting a small sum of money, and where I remained until the 29th, when I left for Red River. I cannot but mention the kindness extended to me by Mr. A. Ludwig and his kind lady, at whose house I stayed four nights.

On the 2nd of April, I arrived at Capt. Finn's on the lost prairie on Red River. From here I went to Marshall's trading house, on Blue River. I succeeded in securing Mr. Marshall's efforts in my behalf, and I purchased his stock of goods, as also the goods of Messrs. Colwell & Wallace, amounting in all to about $1000, with which they agreed to go on to try and purchase the prisoners.

Leaving Mr. Marshall's, I returned to Smith's trading house, and succeeded in securing his goods, subject to my order, provided I should need them in purchasing the prisoners' freedom. Here I met with a Shawnee Indian, from whom I learned that a white woman had been purchased by Mr. Sprawling, one of Mr. Marshall's traders. I immediately returned to Marshall's, who, having heard the same news, had started out the day before my arrival, and had left for me the following note:

"My Friend, James W. Parker,

Sir:—Having received good news, I start after the prisoner tomorrow morning. Mr. Sprawling has purchased a woman; I hope it is your daughter. Keep yourself here. The Comanches are now at Coffee's. You must stay here until I come back, and if God spares my life I will have the prisoners. I have got three Indians engaged at two dollars per day. For God Almighty's sake stay here until I come back, and see what can be done.

In haste, your friend,
SAMUEL B. MASHALL.

April, 1837."

It will be discovered by Marshall's note, that he was extremely anxious that I should remain at his trading house until his return. This grew out of his fears that I would venture among the Indians, in which event he knew I would be killed. Under these circumstances, who of my readers that ever felt in his breast the pure and holy vibrations of paternal love, could have commanded himself in obedience to the more cautious and calm requirements of one, who though he might feel all the interest benevolence and philanthropy could prompt, yet felt comparatively nothing. Can it be supposed then that I obeyed his directions? I did not; for I immediately started for the traders' camp, where I supposed my daughter was. When I arrived at the camp, I was chagrined to learn that the woman was not my daughter. I remained with the traders several days, exerting every means to regain my child, but to no effect.

It was now the 21st of April, and having lost all hope of regaining my daughter by the plan I had laid, I determined to go among the Indians and reconnoitre their camps, with the hopes of seeing her, and by stealth effecting her release. With this view, I prepared myself with a good rifle, four pistols and a bowie knife, a sufficient quantity of ammunition, and pen, ink and paper. I would remark, that, knowing it was the custom of the Indians to make their prisoners carry all the water, and knowing that they never encamped but on the bank of a river or creek, my plan was, after discovering their encampment, to keep myself concealed until dark, and then while they were dancing, as is their custom every night after dark, to creep to the point from whence they procured their water, and having written notes directing any American into whose hands they might fall, where to come to me, to place them in positions where they would be likely to be found, and after doing this, to return to my hiding place. In this way, I hoped to get a note in to the hands of my daughter, and thus effect her release.

I accordingly started in company with one of the men belonging to a trading house, and we directed our course for the camps of the Comanches. On the 24th, having stopped for the night and hobbled our horses, we lay down, but we very soon found that we were among the Indians, and that they were trying to steal our horses. I immediately sprang to my feet, and I discovered an Indian not more than ten feet from me. I shot him with my rifle and fired at another with my pistol. He immediately ran off, and we, mounting our horses, followed his example.

We rode all night. The next day at ten o'clock, we came upon a company of Indians in ambush. We did not know that they were near us until the crack of their rifles and the stinging of my left ear and cheek from the graze of a ball, announced our perilous situation. As quick as thought, I had my trusty rifle to my shoulder, and seeing a very large Indian a few yards to my left, with his empty rifle yet to his face, I fired. He made no effort to rise, and my attention being directed to another spot, I saw another Indian preparing to fire a second time. I drew one of my pistols and fired it. He appeared to come to the conclusion not to fire a second time, for he immediately laid down as if to take some rest. My companion during this time had induced the third Indian to forego a second fire; and having no further business to transact at that particular spot, and hearing a short distance off a yell as if all the demons of hell were around us, we left, without taking time to wish our three friends in ambush a comfortable rest and pleasant dreams. Nor did we wait to select our course; but, urging our faithful horses to do their duty, we soon left our pursuers far behind.

On the 26th, my companion left me and started for the trading house. I swam the Ouachita, or Cash Fork of Red River, and left my horse, finding that I could proceed on foot with less danger than on horseback. I then swam Red River and found the Indians.

I reconnoitred them until the second of June, practising all the plans I had arranged without being able to make any discoveries. Being now almost exhausted, having reconnoitred the Indians more than a month, during which time I had gone without food as long as six days at one time, and often four or five days, I determined to return home. It is probably necessary to remark, that when I did eat any thing, I had to go a sufficient distance from the Indians to prevent them from hearing the report of my gun whenever I shot a buffalo. Sometimes, when the Indians moved, I would wait until they had proceeded some eight or ten miles, and then kill my game and satisfy my hunger.

The limits to which I have prescribed this narrative prevent me from relating many interesting incidents that occurred in this and the other tours I made in search of my daughter; but I must relate one here, and leave the reader to picture to himself many similar ones.

One evening after the Indians had moved, but not to a sufficient distance to be out of hearing of my gun, and being very hungry, I shot a buffalo, and proceeded to the bank of a stream not far off, where I kindled a fire for the purpose of broiling a piece of meat. On returning to the buffalo, I found my right to it disputed—not by an Indian, but by a very large white wolf, peculiar only to this section of country. I tried to scare him away, but he was bold and determined, and often cautioned me not to trust too much to his good humor, by showing me the length and condition of his long tusks. I was afraid to shoot a second time, as the Indians doubtless heard the first report, and were perhaps, listening to catch the sound of another.

23

Finding, however, that his wolfship was not to be moved by menaces, and my hunger increasing as the opportunity of satisfying it was before me, I determined after a long time to risk another fire, and accordingly gave my ungenerous companion of the wilderness a leaden pill to work off the hearty supper he had made on my buffalo. Luckily the Indians did not hear the report of my gun, and after having sated my craving appetite, I lay down and had a good night's rest.

On many other occasions when I was afraid to shoot game, I have carried water in my hat a considerable distance to drown out the prairie dogs from their burrows, and in this way procured the food that kept me from starving.

Having returned to the Cash Forks of Red River, and procured my horse, I returned home, after an absence of five months. On the 19th of June, I arrived at the city of Houston, and on the same day Gen Houston gave me the commission of the Commander-in-Chief of a military company, to be denominated the "Independent Volunteers of Texas," without limit as to numbers.

It now being evident that the Indians would not enter into a treaty, President Houston had at last agreed to order an expedition against them; and I, as above stated, having been honored with the command of the expedition, immediately set about raising a company of volunteers for that purpose.

CHAPTER IV.

I raise a company—the false impressions made on Gen. Houston's mind as to my intentions—I receive orders from Gen. Houston to abandon the Expedition against the Indians, and to disband my troops—an account of similar tours to those spoken of in the previous chapter, among the Indians.

My brother, Nathaniel Parker, of Charleston, Ill., then and now a member of the Senate of that State, had arrived in Texas; and assisted by him and my brother Joseph, I soon succeeded in raising a company of as brave men as that young republic could boast. My arrangements were fast being matured for an effective expedition against the Indians, when to my great surprise and mortification, I received orders from Gen. Houston to abandon the expedition and to disband the company I had partly raised! It appears that he was induced to do this by the misrepresentations of some evil disposed persons. He had been made to believe that I premeditated an attack upon some friendly and well-disposed Indian tribes near the frontier of Texas; which was entirely destitute of truth, as the testimony of Col. Jos. Williams, Daniel Montague, N. Parker, Majors William Lloyd and W. T. Henderson, and many others, all worthy men, will clearly prove.

My brother Nathaniel finding he could render me no assistance, returned home to Illinois. Brother Joseph and myself disbanded the men, but went ourselves into the Indian territory, determined to try what we could do.

We had traveled about 500 miles, when from the excessive heat and the want of proper food and water, we were both taken sick and compelled to return home, where we arrived on the 31st of August.

On the 7th of September, having partially recovered from my indisposition, I started again on another tour, with as firm a determination never to cease my efforts until the prisoners were released, as I had formed when I first started in pursuit of them.

This tour was a long and painful one to me, owing to the bad state of my health; though nothing of interest to the reader occurred. Finding my indisposition increasing, I was again compelled to return to my family.

After remaining at home four or five days, and my health

becoming better, I again left home on the 27th of October, and went to see if the Indian traders whom I had engaged, had done or learned any thing. Finding they had done nothing, nor learned any tidings of my daughter, I pursued my course among the Indian tribes, then on the frontier of the United States. On arriving at an Indian town, I would stop and make inquiries for my daughter.

At one of these towns I met with an Indian who had on one of my vests. I told one of my companions that if it was my vest, the button moulds were made of the rind of a gourd; and to decide whether it was in truth my vest, I cut off one of the buttons, and soon recognized it as having been made by my own hands at Fort Parker. I interrogated the Indian as to where he procured the vest, and he being unable to give me a definite account of it—the treacherous capture of Fort Parker—the inhuman butchery of my aged father and my affectionate brothers—the galling captivity and slavish bondage of my dear child and innocent and helpless grand-children and nieces—all, rushed upon my mind at the same moment, and the firm belief that this was one of the authors of all my woe, kindled in my breast feelings that I leave the reader to imagine, for my pen cannot describe them. Every nerve of my system involuntarily trembled, and I felt it was necessary that I should leave the town; so directing my companions to start on, assuring them that I would soon follow *with all possible speed*, I mounted my horse, and taking a "last, fond look" at my vest—*with one eye through the sight of my trusty rifle*—I "turned and left the spot," with the assurance that my vest *had got a new button hole!*

The Indians of the town, as I passed them, appeared desirous that I should make a longer stay, which was manifested by their frequent attempts to catch my bridle and in other ways to arrest my progress; but some well aimed blows with my sword soon cleared the track, and my spirited steed quickly bore me beyond their reach. On coming up with my companions, we pursued our journey without further molestation.

We soon reached Sabine River, and having crossed it, entered an Indian town. The Indians at this town were drinking whiskey very freely when we arrived, and many were intoxicated. We soon found that our safety required as short a stay here as possible, and therefore did not alight from our horses. Just as we were about to start, an Indian, evidently much intoxicated, seized my bridle and drew a knife. I soon found it necessary

26

for my own safety, to knock him down with my rifle, in doing which it was broken and rendered useless. Now, it was necessary that we should, not only leave immediately, but flee for our lives, as the Indians had become enraged and were rushing to attack us. We soon left them far behind, and we pursued the remainder of our journey homeward without molestation.

I arrived at home, from this tour, on the 28th of October. Finding that my health was much impaired from traveling, I started my son-in-law, (Mr. Nixon,) to see what my traders had done. On the 30th of November at a late hour of the night, a Mr. G. S. Parks arrived at my house, and informed me that he had met Mr. Nixon, and that he had directed him to go on to Independance, Missouri, where Mrs. Plummer was, she having been brought into that place by some Santa Fe traders.

Reader, I leave you to your own conceptions of what were my feelings on hearing this joyful news. My wife rushed eagerly to my side to hear the glad tidings, and so overjoyed was she to hear that her child was yet alive, that she fell, senseless, in my arms, whilst my little children gathered around me, all anxiously inquiring: "Father, does sister Rachel still live?"

How chequered are the ways of Providence. Though my sorrows and sufferings, for the past two years, had been greater than it would be thought human nature could bear, the joy I felt that night overbalanced them all, whilst I poured forth to Almighty God, the humble thanks of a grateful heart for the merciful deliverance of my child from a cruel bondage. How truly does the inspired writer say, that He chasteneth when it seemeth fit, and maketh the sorrowful heart to rejoice in due season.

On the 19th of February, Mr. Nixon and Mrs. Plummer arrived at my house, and great indeed was the joy on her return to the bosom of her friends. She presented a most pitiable appearance; her ematiated body was covered with scars, the evidences of the savage barbarity to which she had been subject during her captivity.

She was in very bad health, and although every thing was done to restore her, she lived but a short time to enjoy the company of her kind husband and affectionate relatives. In about one year from the time she returned to her paternal home, she calmly breathed out her spirit to Him who gave it, and her friends committed her body to the silent grave.

During her protracted illness, she was seldom heard to murmur at her own sufferings, past or present, which she knew would soon end; but her whole soul appeared continually engaged in prayer to God for the preservation and deliverance of her dear and only child, James Pratt, from the inhuman bondage he was suffering. She often said that this life had no charms for her, and that her only wish was, that she might live to see her son restored to his friends. Although she was denied this happiness, I rejoice to feel that her prayers were heard and answered, in the deliverance of her child, as the following chapter discloses.

For a full account of her sufferings, during her captivity, the reader is referred to her own narrative which is appended to and closes this volunme.

CHAPTER V.

*I hear of two children having been brought into the Chickasaw
Depot, which I suppose are my grandson and nephew. I go
to see them—narrow escape from the Indians—return home
—hear of the children at Fort Gibson—go after them and
bring them home.*

Having recovered my daughter, and not feeling certain that
my grandson and my brother's children were yet alive, I partially ceased my exertions to regain them. I, however, let no
opportunity escape, where I thought there was the least prospect
of hearing of them. I also made a tour once a year through
the Indian country in search of them, but could hear nothing
certain about them until the first of September, 1841, when I
heard that two children had been brought into the Chickasaw
Depot, about 800 miles from my house. At this time I was very
sick with a fever; but in hopes that I might be able to reach the
Depot, and thinking that traveling might perhaps help me, I
started. I was scarcely able to mount my mule, when I started,
yet it is no less strange than true that I traveled fifty miles the
first day.

When I got among the Indians, I found that I was in great
danger, owing to some difficulties that had taken place between
the frontier Texans and the Chickasaw and Choctaw tribes of
Indians. It was necessary, therefore, that I should pass myself
as a citizen of Arkansas, in order to pass unmolested. I succeeded in reaching the Depot on the 22nd of September. There
were many Indians at the Depot when I arrived, and to my horror I found that many of them were of the same tribe to which
the Indian belonged that had on my vest, the particulars of
which are previously related.

Maj. Jones, the chief proprietor of the Depot, I found to be a
gentleman and a friend, and to him I communicated the object of
my visit. He informed me that the children that had been
brought in were not those I was looking for, but said that his
traders knew of some children among the Comanches that no
doubt were those I was in search of. His traders were just
about starting when I arrived, and he called in two of the head
men and directed them to purchase these children at any price,
becoming himself responsible for the amount they might cost.

One of these traders, an old Delaware, with whom I was

well acquainted, took me aside and told me that I was in danger, and pointed out an Indian in the crowd who had said I had killed his brother. This Indian was probably a brother of the one that had on my vest. After the traders had started, Maj. Jones gave me the same caution that old Frank, the Delaware, had given me, and added, that he would invite me to stay at the Depot that night, but he knew if I stayed the Indians would steal my mule.

Soon after Maj. Jones had left me, the Indian pointed out to me by the old trader, stepped up to me and asked, with apparent unconcern, if I was going to leave that evening? I replied I was. He asked me which road I was going? I told him the Fort Towson road. He then left me, and I saw him conversing with his companions.

Well acquainted, as I was, with the Indian character, it cannot be supposed that I was not perfectly aware of the danger I was in. In this case, as in all my other difficulties with the Indians, I was not the least alarmed. I mean, I was perfectly in possession of my presence of mind, and could control my feelings and actions so entirely, that I was enabled to act for the best. To remain at the Depot I knew would be inexpedient, as the Indians would steal my mule, and then all hopes of escape would be cut off. So there was but one alternative left, and that was to start home.

Soon after the Indian above spoken of, had interrogated me, I saw him and forty or fifty others mount their mules and start down the road I was compelled to travel. I studied a few moments on the best course to pursue, and after they had been gone about one hour, I started. I had observed as I came up the Fort Towson road, a very heavy ambush about two miles from the Depot, where I was sure these Indians intended to kill me. The road forked about half way between the Depot and this ambush, the right hand fork leading to Blue river. This road I determined to take, and thus avoid the ambush. I was entirely unarmed, and I knew that my only means of escape was in flight. Just as I came to the forks of the road I met two of these Indians, who had no doubt returned to watch me, and if I had taken the Blue river road I am confident they would have shot me; so I was compelled to go the Fort Towson road. Soon after I met them I observed that they turned round and followed me. I was about two hundred yards ahead of them and was nearly in sight of the ambush, when a short turn in the

30

road concealed me from their view. I now turned short to the right. and urging my mule with whip and spur, I was soon out of sight of the road, and crossing the Blue river road, took a straight direction through a boggy prairie. I did not slacken my pace until I had gone seven or eight miles, but kept looking behind to ascertain if I was pursued. I was now near a high piece of land, that bordered on the prairie, and in order to let my mule rest, and to ascertain whether I was pursued, I went to the most elevated point near me, and reconnoitered the prairie as far as I could see. I soon discovered the whole body of Indians, about two miles behind, running directly towards me. Remounting my mule, and applying whip and spur, I urged him, at full speed, for nearly two hours. Having arrived at the foot of a mountain, and there being no point in sight but what appeared insurmountable, I almost despaired of escaping. As there was no time for delay, I started to climb the mountain, which I succeeded in doing, after much labor and great danger to myself and mule. When I reached the top, the sun was just setting, and my mule being very tired, I permitted him to rest, while I climbed a tree, to see if the Indians were still pursuing me; I could see nothing of them, and concluded they had given up the chase. Descending the tree, I was soon on my way, and directing my course so as to intersect the Blue river road, which I gained about twelve o'clock that night, and about two in the morning crossed Blue river, where I found a good hiding place and lay down and slept until day-break, when I pursued my journey and was soon out of all danger from the Indians.

I have not narrated here all my plans and difficulties in making my escape; but enough has been said to induce my readers to agree with me in ascribing the preservation of my life to the protecting care of a kind Providence.

Nothing further of interest transpired in this tour. I arrived at home on the 8th of October. My family and friends were as much grieved as myself, at my disappointment in not finding the children.

Having learned from the public papers, and otherwise, that two children had been brought in to Fort Gibson, I started for that place on the 22nd of December, 1842. Nothing of note occurred on this journey. I arrived at Fort Gibson on the 15th of January, 1843, where I was rejoiced to find my grandson, James Pratt Plummer, and my nephew, John Parker.

I found Capt. Brown, the commandant of the Fort, a perfect gentleman. He treated me very kindly, and rendered me all the aid necessary. I soon convinced him that the children were those I was in search of.

When the children were brought to me, although seven years had elapsed since I had seen them, and they had altered very much by growth, and from the ill usage of the Indians, I recognized in the features of my grandson, those of his mother, Mrs. Plummer; and my joy at rescuing him from Indian barbarity was not a little abated by the reminisences brought to mind by his striking resemblance of his mother. The sympathising officers of the garrison appeared to partake of the mingled feelings of joy and grief, it was beyond my power to restrain on the occasion.

My grandson, learning that I had come after him, ran off, and went to the Dragoon encampment, about one mile from the Garrison. Poor child, how my heart bled, when he thus avoided me. Torn, as he had been, in his infancy, from the tender care of a mother and father; unused, as he had been, (until he arrived at this place) to enjoying kind treatment from anybody; ignorant, as he was, of any of those tender feelings of love and kind attentions which are the offspring of paternal affection, it is not to be thought strange that he was incapable of appreciating my kind intentions toward him.

Being much fatigued, I retired to rest, but my sufferings and trials for the last seven years, passing in retrospect across my mind, sleep was driven from my eyes, and I arose in the morning but little refreshed.

Early the next morning Capt. Brown sent a Sergeant after my grandson. When he arrived, the Captain and some of the other officers joined with me in persuading him to go with me. After more than two hours conversation, we succeeded in making him understand how I was related to him, at which he appeared much astonished, and asked me if he had a mother. I told him he had not, as she had died. He then asked if he had a father. I told him he had, and if he would go with me he should see him. He then consented to accompany me.

It will be recalled that the children were very young when taken by the Indians, and consequently could now talk very little English. As I could not well understand them, nor they me, I was relieved from the pain of listening to their recital of the sufferings they had endured whilst among the Indians. The

32

evidences, however, of the free exercise of savage barbarity, were visible upon the backs of these unfortunate children; for there was scarcely a place wherever the finger could be laid, without its covering a scar made by the lash.

After these children became able to make themselves understood, their own recital of their sufferings would make any heart bleed.

Capt. Brown made out the necessary documents to the Executive of Texas, and we were soon on our way home. The two boys rode my horse, and I walked, until we reached Fort Smith. Finding that I could walk no farther, I here purchased a pony. We now pursued our journey, and a severe time we had of it. The children, as well as myself, were very thinly clad; and there having been a heavy fall of rain, we found the road in many places almost impassable. Added to this, the weather was very cold; and we all suffered very much. Soon after we crossed Red River, one of our horses was bogged, and it was sometime in the night before we succeeded in getting him out.

We arrived at home on the 27th of February, much fatigued. My wife and many of my neighbors met me at Cincinnati, on the Trinity River, twelve miles from my house, and joyous indeed was our meeting. I had now completed another tour of suffering; and grateful were my feelings to God on finding myself again with my family, and all in good health.

The boys soon became attached to me and my family. They soon learned to speak English, and are now doing well.

I cannot close this chapter without an acknowledgment of the kind treatment I received from many persons in going to and returning from Fort Gibson; among whom I would name Capt. Rogers and Capt. Bliss, of Fort Smith; Col. Lumas, of Fort Towson; Parson Potts, missionary among the Choctaws; and Mr. Donoho, of Clarksville.

CHAPTER VI.

A brief synopsis of the foregoing chapters—I hear of a girl having been brought into Jasper County, Missouri, whom I start to see, thinking she was my niece Cynthia Ann Parker —my disappointment—I go to Charleston, Illinois—thence to Louisville, Kentucky.

In writing out the foregoing chapters, which cover the most interesting part of my narrative, it has been necessary to abridge as much as possible. In doing this, many interesting events and amusing anecdotes have unavoidably been omitted for want of space. To enter minutely into all the particulars, and to re-hearse all that transpired in my journeyings in seach of the prisoners, would occupy, at least, three hundred pages; the expense of printing which I am not able to bear. Another reason for omitting a detail of many of my sufferings and miraculous escapes, is, that I am confident few, of any, would believe them.

The reader no doubt thinks that what I have already related of my sufferings is miraculous enough; but, could I retrace my life, and endure again my past sufferings, and make him an eye-witness to them, then he would agree with me, that what I have narrated is nothing, when compared with the awful reality.

From the capture of the Fort, up to the time my daughter was recovered, at least three-fourths of my time was spent in the wilderness. Sometimes I would not see a human being, except Indians, and they at a distance off, for two months. My only food was wild meat, without salt or bread, and that often un-cooked. My only resting place, the cold ground; and my only covering, the arched dome of Heaven. Often I was without a mouthful of food for five or six days at a time; and frequently hope fled my bosom, and despair, horrible despair seized upon me. More than twenty times have I calmly and sincerely wished that death would end my sufferings; and on one or two occa-sions, I was on the eve of aiding the fell monster in the work with my own hands.

My feet being very tender, from freezing, I could often have been traced by the blood that marked my every step over the frozen ground. Sometimes, in the heat of summer, whilst re-connoitering the Indians in the large prairies, the vertical rays of the mid-day sun would so blister and parch my face and hands, that the skin would peel from them; and often my thirst was so great, that I would have given a mountain of pure gold, had I possessed it, for one draught of water.

Most of the country over which I traveled, was infested by beasts of prey and venomous reptiles; and not unfrequently have I narrowly escaped being destroyed by the ravenous jaws of the former, or the venomous fangs of the latter.

My readers may feel some surprise that I always went on these tours alone. A moment's reflection will convince them of the propriety of my doing so. I was not permitted to take a sufficient number of men with me to fight the Indians, and my only hope was to steal the prisoners from the enemy. The fewer in company then, less was the danger of my being discovered by the savages and killed. But, to return to a continuation of my narrative.

In February, 1844, information was received in Texas that a girl had been purchased from the Comanches and brought to Jasper county, Missouri, who, from the description given of her, I thought was my niece, now the only prisoner that was taken at Fort Parker, that had not been recovered.

I procured my passport from the Executive of Texas, and set about arranging my affairs for a journey to Missouri to see this girl. I first tried to raise some money, but although I offered to sell property for one-tenth of its real value, for that purpose, I failed. I tried to borrow money from Gen. Houston, and others, but there was scarcely any money in the country, and consequently all my endeavors to raise funds availed me nothing. Having prepared to start, I determined to wait no longer for money; and on the 21st day of June took leave of my family, assuring them that this should be the last journey I would go in pursuit of the prisoner.

When I reached Clarksville, in Texas, I stopped a few days for the purpose of getting some money due me there. I collected five dollars. When that was expended, I solicited work that I might get some more, but could find no one who had money to pay for the kind of work I could do.

I now pursued my journey to Missouri; and although I had but a few dollars, it is no less strange than true, that it was as much as I needed. On my whole route, the people whom I met treated me with a kindness and liberality I little looked for from entire strangers. It is true that to many of them I was personally a stranger; yet, they knew me well by character.

With the exception of the extreme warm weather, and much annoyance from the horse flies in the western part of Arkansas and Missouri, I had a pleasant journey. I reached Jasper county, Missouri, on the 5th of August, and found that the girl I went to see was not my niece, but, as I believed, the daughter of a Mrs. Williams of Texas. I proposed to take her with me to Texas, on my return, which created some unpleasant feelings between one of the citizens of that county and myself. However, I resolved that she should accompany me to Texas on my return.

Having learned that there was a white girl among the Kickapoo Indians, I determined to go to see her, and accordingly set out for that purpose. I arrived at Maj. Robert Cummins' (Indian Agent,) near Westport, Missouri, on the 15th of August. Maj. C., as soon as I presented him my authority from my Government, set out with me to the Kickapoo nation. We went by the way of Fort Leavenworth, and the stationed officers there promptly rendered all the necessary aid. We soon found the girl, who proved to be of the same nation of Indians, but having some white blood in her. They wished to pass her off as a white girl for the purpose of gain.

To Maj. Cummins I am under lasting obligations for his prompt attention to my call, as well as many signal favors rendered me.

On the 20th of August, I put an advertisement in the "Western Expositor," published at Independence, Missouri, offering a reward of $300 for any prisoner that might be brought in, and $500 for my niece. Having enlisted the good feelings of several of the leading men of Independence in my favor, and secured the assistance of Col. Alvaier, the U. S. Minister to Santa Fe, Dr. Waldo, and Maj. Rickman, in forwarding my object, I determined to go to brother Nathaniel Parker's, in Charleston, Illinois.

On this route, as well as the one from Texas to Independence, I had many interesting meetings. I attended the Mount Gilead Association, 35 miles from Quincy, Ill., where I had the pleasure of cultivating an acquaintance with many of the brethren, among among whom were Elders Harper, Hogan, Roberts, Williams, Dr. James M. Clarkson, and many others. I reached my brother's, in Charleston, on the 20th of September. I remained sometime in that county; and it was here my friends again urged upon me to have my journal published.

Here I met with Elder B. B. Piper, who urged me to accompany him to Louisville, and proffered me all the aid in his power in getting the work through the press. We arrived in Louisville on the 18th day of October. I have found in Louisville a magnanimous people, among whom I have found *friends indeed*. Among those from whom I have received particular kindnesses, and to whom I shall ever feel under obligations, I cannot forego naming Mr. and Mrs. Kennedy, Mrs. Breckenridge, Mr. A. L. Shotwell and lady, Mr. W. N. Haldeman, Mr. R. B. J. Twyman and lady, and Mr. J. M. Stephens and lady.

In Sellersburg, Indiana, I have also met with many kind friends, whose favors I shall remember with the most lively gratitude, among whom I could name Elder M. W. Sellers, Mr. Wm. Jackson, Mr. Sparks and Mr. Wm. Parker.

Since I have been in Louisville, I have tried, under much affliction, to preach. I have also visited several of the neighboring churches—at New Albany, Sellersburg, Elk Creek, Buckrun, &c. I hope, through the mercy of Providence, soon to be on my home, where I shall endeavor to spend the remainder of my days in the faithful discharge of my duty to my God, my country and my family.

JAMES W. PARKER.

Picture of Cyntha Ann Parker, with her babe nursing, Prairie
Flower, taken a few days after her capture by Sull
Ross, mother of Quanna Parker, Comanche
Indian Chief.

Geographical Description
of the
Climate, Soil, Timber Water, &c.,
—of—
TEXAS

Texas it situated between 29 and 42 degrees N. lat., and 16½ and 24 degrees W. lon., from Washington city.

It is bordered on the north and east by the United States; south, by the Gulf of Mexico; west, by the Rio Grande, (Big River;) thence by a direct northern line to 42 degrees N. lat. At 32 degrees N. lat., the line between Texas and the United States strikes Red River, not far from the Sulphur Fork, and a short distance above the Great Raft. Ascending this river, I shall only notice the country on the Texas side. There are many small tributaries, but none of note, until we reach the Bois d'arc, which takes its name from the abundance of that timber growing on its banks.

The bottoms on Red River are generally rich; but, owing to the overflows to which they are subject, much the largest portion of them are valueless. The small streams that empty themselves into Red River, through these streams, are almost impassable, on account of the bogs that border them nearly their whole length. In these bottoms are also many small lakes and ponds, which, with the low, marshy condition of that section of the country, render it very unhealthy, and make it an unfit residence for man. Mosquitoes are plentiful here; and healthy water for family use is not to be found.

The soil is mostly of a dark red sticky clay, which is very hard when dry. Yet there are many fine farms in a high state of cultivation in these bottoms, and great quantities of cotton and corn are grown. In the course of time, when the river has levees built on its banks and the ponds are drained, nearly all these bottoms will become valuable. There are some prairies in these bottoms—Lost prairie, Eelom's prairie, Jonesborough, &c. The bottoms are generally from a mile and a half to three miles wide; and in some places the river is banked by the high lands. At Old Spanish Bluff, a few miles above Lost Prairie, there is a good site for a town. Upon the high lands the timber is generally oak and hickory, interspersed with pine. The soil is generally of a sandy quality—in some places, of a dark loam appearance; in others, of a whiter color. In wet weather seasons, these ridges are very boggy and almost impassable.

In the Red River bottoms the timber grows very heavy, and consists of a variety. Oak, ash, gum, elm, walnut, pecan, Bois d'arc, &c. The Bois d'arc is a very valuable timber, as it partakes somewhat of the qualities of lignum vitae. When well seasoned, it can only be worked with a file. There are many springs of excellent water found among the high lands bordering on the bottoms.

The range for stock is tolerably good; the grass on the high lands furnishing food in summer, and the cane in the bottoms supplying the same in winter. The high floods are often dangerous to the cattle and hogs; and many are lost by getting into swamps and becoming bogged.

Farther out from the river, where the small streams have their beginning, the face of the country is level, and generally poor land. It is very dangerous to travel through that part of the country in a wet season, as in many places the ground presents a solid appearance to the eye, when if you venture upon it, your horse will bog beyond all recovery in a moment's time. The timber is mostly post oak and pine on the hills; whilst on the borders of the creeks, it is principally black walnut, red oak and hickory.

The country from Red River to Sulphur Fork, partakes generally of the character of that above described. It is fast settling; and although to the passing traveler the country is not prepossessing, yet it produces remarkably well. Villages are fast springing up, farms being opened daily, and this country bids fair to be densely inhabited in a short time.

Pecan Creek heads in a large prairie, which continues in a westerly direction between Sulphur Fork and main Red River. This prairie is very rich. In it is located the flourishing town of Clarksville, the county seat of Red River County. The stranger would be struck with the beauty of this town, situated as it is in a fine farming country, and surrounded by the most valuable farms in a high state of cultivation. There are several stores, taverns, and other business houses, in Clarksville, and nearly all the mechanical branches are also carried on. The "Northern Standard," edited by Maj. Demorse, is published here. The town is growing very fast; and although the spot on which it

40

stands was a trackless wilderness ten years since, it now numbers about 1000 inhabitants. What it will be ten years hence, it is impossible to conjecture.

Blossom prairie, a few miles west of Clarksville, is not surpassed for luxuriance of soil and salubrity of climate, by any section of country it was ever my good fortune to travel over. In the south border of this prairie is located the seat of justice of Lamar county. The town, I believe, is yet without a name. This prairie is about 30 miles along and 6 in width. The section of country between this prairie and Red River, is of a superior quality to that on Pecan Bayou, (or creek,) being more free from bogs. It is mostly a prairie country, continuing west from Clarksville, until we reach the head of Sulphur Fork and Bois d'arc rivers. The soil and timber on these rivers are much the same, and not unlike those on Pecan Bayou.

The face of the country near the mouth of Bois d'arc River, is very similar to that around Jonesborough. There are not as many lakes and ponds found there; but the soil and timber are alike. The distance from Jonesborough to the spot where the Bois d'arc empties inself into Red River, is about 60 miles. About twenty miles from its mouth, the Bois d'arc looses its channel, and passes promiscuously through a bottom of some 6 miles in length and two miles in width. This place is called the "Scatters." When the river is full, this bottom presents one general lake; and in a very dry season, the bottom is entirely dry. A few miles above this place is Fort English, the seat of justice of Fannin County. About twenty miles from this, on Red River, is the town of Warren, formerly the seat of justice. It is on the south side of Red River. Col Daniel Montague is the proprietor. A few miles above this town, Choctaw Bayou empties its waters into Red River. This bayou drains a mountainous country. The country bordering on Red River below is very badly watered.

Immediately above Warren, and at several points between there and the mouth of Bos d'arc River, are very high bluffs, which, from the varied colors of the stone of which they are formed, present a singular and picturesque appearance. Some of the rocks are perfectly white, some red, and others black. A few miles above this are the Cross Timbers, which will be described in another place. For many miles above this point, the country is hilly and very broken. The timber grows very thick and of

41

nearly all kinds. There are many fine mill sites to be found, and the bottoms are very rich. In these bottoms, cane and green briars grow in abundance.

False Ouachita River empties itself into Red River at the Cross Timbers, from the north side. The course of Red River for some miles below this point, is E. N. E.; but a few miles above, the Texas line will leave the Red River and run due North to Arkansas River. This line is to run 100 degrees W. lon. from Greenwich. Here is a large and desirable country that belongs to Texas, that has, as yet, received but little attention. This country, which is drained by False Ouachita and other tributaries of Red River, on the one side; and by Canadian, Arkansas, &c., on the other, is well diversified; being well watered, and timbered with oak, ash, walnut, hickory, hackberry, &c., and very rich. There are some few prairies. The country is now inhabited by the Choctaws, Chickasaws, and other tribes of friendly Indians. When this country becomes settled, it will be found as healthy as any in the world, as there exist no local causes to produce disease.

At the mouth of the Cash Fork of Witchataw River, Red River is so hemmed in by impassable mountains, that it is impossible at present to find egress to the back country; but as we ascend the river, the country becomes more level and fine, rich prairies are now found. This is a fine wheat growing country and there is no doubt that the day is near at hand when the wheat grown on these prairies will supply the whole interior of Texas.

In all this section of country, wild honey may be found in abundance, and when it is settled it may truly be called the land that "flows with milk and honey." As an evidence of the great quantity of honey to be found in this section of the country, it is not unusual to find, where timber is scarce, bee-hives on the ground in the prairie grass. I found one of these hives, if they may be so called, in one of my tours. The outside of the little house is covered with a kind of wax, which, whilst it is impervious to water, the heat of the sun has no effect upon it. When I found this I cut a hole in it, and took as much honey as I could eat. Sometime after, when passing that way, I again visited it, and found the industrious inmates of this little house had repaired the breach I had wantonly made, and were pursuing their labors as usual. The honey was too tempting and I again regaled myself upon the sweet product of their labor. These

42

waxen honey castles will withstand snows and rains and the hottest rays of the sun; and when they escape the ravages of the greedy bear (this animal is very fond of honey, and never suffers an opportunity for satiating his appetite to pass,) and the raging fire of the burning prairie, they will stand for several years. But to turn from this digression.

The Sulphur Fork of Red River heads in Fannin county. This is a heavy running deep stream, and runs parallel with main Red River, at an average distance of about thirty-five miles. The country between these two rivers has already been described.

Southwest of Sulphur Fork, that is, between it and Cypress creek, there is a high rolling tract of country abounding in iron ore of the richest quality. Springs are plenty here, but the water is so strongly impregnated with iron that it is very disagreeable to the taste. The town of Dangerfield is situated between Sulphur Fork and Big Cypress. In this section of country the timber is diversified, and the soil is much better than that described on the opposite side of the river, with the exception of Blossom prairie and the adjacent country. The bottoms on this river, like those on Red River, are boggy. The bed of the river partakes so much of the character of its bottoms and banks, that it is impossible to ford it, even in the dryest time, except at a few places. The land near the mouth of Sulphur Fork is so low that it often overflows, in consequence of which it will doubtless never be settled.

White Oak Creek, which takes its name from the abundance of that timber found on its banks, empties into Sulphur Fork nearly opposite Clarksville. It drains a fine tract of country. Here is a large settlement, as there is also east and south of this. The soil here, although productive, is also boggy. Good water is seldom found, though no doubt, as the country becomes settled the water will improve.

Big and Little Cypress do not reach the Cross Timbers. They stand second among the small streams of Texas. There is such a similarity between the land on these creeks and that just described, that a few remarks will suffice. There are few prairies found here, and those very small. The soil is rather wet, though much of it is very rich. The timber is very heavy, particularly south of Little Cypress, and in the vicinity of Soda Lake. It consists mostly of cypress, oak, ash, elm, hickory,

43

walnut and pine. Shumake, red bud, buckeye, and in short, all the undergrowth usually found in the Western states grow in abundance here.

This section of country is now thickly settled; and the flourishing town of Marshal, the seat of justice of Harrison county, having sprung up as by magic, being located in its center, is making rapid strides to distinction among her sister towns of this young Republic. This country, a few years since was held by the Caddo Indians; and the weary traveler, as he pursued his lonesome way, was in continued danger of savage barbarity. There are now several stores, two or three public houses, &c., &c., at Marshal, and it supports an interesting newspaper, called the "Marshal Review." Business of every description appears brisk, and the emigration now flowing into that interesting section of country, is of that class calculated to make it rise, with giant strides, to importance.

On Big Cypress, at the crossing of the Cherokee trace, is located Fort Sherman, whither the citizens of that country would flee in case they were attacked by the Indians. Many persons have been murdered here by the Indians; but it is confidently believed that there is no danger now to be apprehended from the Indians in that part of the country.

There is but a small portion of this region of country that may be called first-rate, though most of it stands high in the second class. There are many fine springs and some good mills in this section of the country. These two streams empty their waters into and form Lake Soda.

The line between Texas and Louisiana crosses this lake about twenty miles from its head. The lake on either side is bordered by large bodies of fine land, and many wealthy farmers have already located and improved the largest portion of it, who annually grow fine crops of cotton, corn, oats, rye, potatoes, barley, &c. This country, as well as all that adjoining large rivers or lakes, (as in all new countries,) is at present sickly. But as it becomes settled the health improves. The sickness is generally chills and fevers.

A line on the 32 degree of north latitude separates this part of Texas from the United States. This line terminates on the southwest bank of the Sabine; and it is this intervening country that I shall now notice.

Sabine river empties its waters into Sabine bay, and is the eastern boundary of Texas, from the Gulf of Mexico to the

44

32nd degree N. latitude. Commencing at the gulf, and ascending the bay, Neytches, (or Snow river,) is the first stream worthy of notice. There are several small creeks that empty into the Sabine below the Texas line—the Pola Cocho, Blue Bayou, Tanaha, &c. Here the country differs very much from any I have described. The soil is of a deep red color, almost rivaling the vermillion hue, and is very productive. The bottom land is generally covered with very heavy cane, is very rich, and were it not for its great liability to overflow, would be very valuable. The creek bottoms are equally as liable to overflow as those on the rivers, as they have very little fall, and their banks being low, the larger streams, when full, overflow the banks of the smaller ones by back water.

The red soil spoken of, runs through the counties of Sabine, Jasper, Shelby, San Augustine, Nacogdoches, and part of Rusk and Houston. There is but little prairie land in this section of the country; timber is abundant, and differs very little in variety from that abounding in the country already described, with the addition of beach, sugar-tree, magnolia, holly and pine. The two latter are found here in great abundance. Mosquitoes and ticks are very numerous, though as the country becomes settled they are less troublesome.

The country lying between the Sabine and Trinity rivers, and north of the San Antonio road, was formerly held by the Cherokee Indians. Many consider this the garden spot of Texas. The face of the country is diversified, so that there can be found in the Cherokee country, any, and almost every variety of land, both as to quality and situation. Some very rich, and some very poor land may be found here. In one spot a fine level prairie, and at another, high undulating heavy timbered land.

The Sabine heads near the Cross Timbers, and drains an extensive and rich country, and is navigable for small class steamboats a distance of 350 or 400 miles. The Cherokee Indians, through their Chief, obtained a grant from the Mexican government, to colonize and settle this country; but becoming jealous of their Chief, (Fields,) they assassinated him before he had organized and arranged the land according to contract, and they occupied the land as a hunting ground, without regard to the fulfillment of the contract specified in the grant, until the year, 1835, when the Provisional Congress being in force, and governing Texas, offered to confirm the grant from the Mexican government to them under certain stipulations, which they failing to comply with, caused their expulsion from the territory. Their removal, however, was not effected until after several hard fought battles.

Snow River empties into Sabine bay a few miles from the mouth of Sabine river. The country between these rivers, for thirty or forty miles, is low, spouty, poor land, with very few exceptions. At or below the junction of the Neytches, and the Angalana rivers, (which forms Snow river,) the country is better, and improves as you ascend. The Angalana drains a large tract of country; having its head in the country lately described as the Cherokee country. I have said that some think this country the "garden spot of Texas." There is much very fine land in this country, but I think it has been greatly over-rated.

The little river Attoeac empties into the Angalana about thirty miles above the junction of the latter with the Neytches. It has its head in Shelby county, and runs through San Augustine county. The country through which it passes is mostly the red soiled land previously spoken of. Iesh Bayou has its beginning in San Augustine county, not far from the city of San Augustine. There are many other small streams tributary to the Angalana, which I shall not notice. The head waters of the Angalana are not far from the Cross Timbers. The country through which it passes is well watered, and generally good land.

This country, since the Indians were driven from it, is fast settling by the whites, many of whom are cultivating the farms improved by the Indians. Some of them have fine peach orchards, and present appearances indicate that the day is not far distant, when this part of Texas will be densely settled. The average distance between the Angalana and Sabine rivers, after ascending either about thirty-five miles, is about fifty miles.

The Neytches river, and the country it drains, are so much like the Angalana and the country just described, that I leave the reader to apply that of the former to the latter. It heads in about the same degree of the Angalana, which is not far from the 33d degree of N. latitude. On this river, in the country claimed and held for a time by the Cherokees, is a fine salt works, which, if properly worked, would furnish salt enough to supply all of Texas. At present it is not worked extensively, because there is not demand for it at a price that will justify the manufacturer. There are many other places on this river, and also on the Angalana, where salt water has been found in

46

abundance. All the head waters of these rivers are strongly impregnated with iron, which is an evidence of the immense quantity of iron ore in this region, which is said, by good judges, to be very rich, particularly on the western or southwestern waters of the Neytches.

On San Pedro bayou are many very rich and large bodies of iron ore and many fine mill sites, on which are some valuable mills. There are many fine farms on this creek. (I would here remark that all the creeks and streams that do not rate as rivers, in Texas are called bayous.)

On Joney creek there are also many fine mill sites. This creek takes its name from the Joney tribe of Indians that once inhabited that section of country. There are many fine springs of good water in this region, and there are but few more healthy countries in the world. This section of country is on the north side of the San Antonio road, in Houston county. Crockett is the seat of Justice for this county, and is a flourishing town. The land on the south side of this road is not so rich as that on the north side; being very level and boggy. There are many prairies here, some of which are very poor, while others are very fertile. It is almost an invariable rule that where you find prairies bordered by pine timber, the land is generally poor; but where it is bordered by post-oak, the land is generally good.

I have now given a general description of that part of Texas bordering on the States of Louisiana and Arkansas embracing the following counies: Fannin, Lamar, Red River, Harrison, Shelby, San Augustine, Sabine and Jasper, and a part of Liberty, Nacogdoches, Houston and Rusk. I will now commence in Jefferson county, at Sabine City, and after describing it, I will, in future, commence at the Gulf of Mexico, with each important stream, as they come, progressing southwest with the gulf stream; and describe each stream from its mouth to its head, and the territory adjacent to and intervening.

SABINE CITY, PASS AND BAY.

Sabine city stands on the south bank of Sabine Pass, immediately where it empties into the Gulf of Mexico. It is a fine healthy situation for a large commercial city, which it is destined to be. It has one of the best harbors on the Gulf of Mexico. At low tide the Pass has fourteen feet of water in it, which gives second class ships easy ingress and egress to the bay. The bay is about forty miles in length, and six miles wide. Ten miles from the city of Sabine, upon a high eminence, there is a United States garrison, from which you have a commanding view of the bay. From this point you may look in a south-westerly direction, and see upon the silver bosom of Sabine bay, the merchant vessels with their snow-white sails, pressed by the gentle breeze, bearing their rich cargoes from foreign countries to this young republic; or having discharged them, and reladen with valuable cargoes of cotton, the produce of the rich soil of Texas, returning to the gulf, where they are soon lost in the distance. Steamboats will also be seen ploughing their way up or down the bay, bearing the rich merchandise of the interior, or valuable produce of the soil to the city of Sabine for exportation. By the aid of a spy-glass, you may look beyond the city, and upon the gulf, and there you may see ships of all classes passing and repassing, all bearing evidence of the healthy state of trade between Texas and the other nations of the earth.

Now go down to the bay, and, in its clear waters, see the thousands of red fish, as they seek for food or playfully glide through their native element. This is the most delicious fish in the world—so say epicures—and may be taken with ease. You will also see immense numbers of porpoise, mullets, and crabs. Along the shores of the bay, may also be found imperishable banks of the most delicious oysters. Wild fowl may be seen in great numbers on this bay, as also on all the principal lakes, bays and streams of Texas. I would here remark, that there is no country, perhaps, on earth, where wild game, from the buffalo down to the squirrel—wild fowl, both water and land—and fish of any quality and number, are more plenty; thus offering a wide field to the hunter and the angler.

Ten miles from this spot, down the bay, you may see the city of Sabine, stretching along the Pass, presenting a most beautiful scene. Now taking a sail-boat, you may soon glide down the bay to the city, and landing, you now stand on the spot, noted in song and in story as the strong hold of La Fitte, the pirate of the Gulf of Mexico. It was here he retreated when pursued by a formidable foe—here he devised his hellish deeds of plunder and murder—here he divided his illgotten wealth among his brave, though outlawed followers, and here the pirates, song mingled with the tempest roar. Many are the tales of hidden treasure here, and a few of its present inhabitants have wasted much time in vain searches after it. Upon this

48

spot, where 20 years ago, revelled this band of pirates, for a long time the terror of the Gulf, there is now rising, in grandeur and magnificence, a commercial city, which is destined, at no distant day, to rival any other on the American continent.

The gulf-breeze renders a residence in this city both pleasant and healthy. Already have extensive commercial houses been established here, and mechanics are fast filling the city with shops.

GALVESTON CITY, ISLAND AND BAY—TRINITY RIVER, AND LIBERTY COUNTY

Leaving Sabine city, we will sail along the coast, and at a distance of about ninety miles, reach the city of Galveston, which numbers about 9,000 inhabitants. This city is situated on Galveston Island, which is formed by Galveston Bay on the North, the Gulf of Mexico on the East and South, and by West Bay, on the West. The Island is about 25 miles in length, and its average width is about five miles. The city of Galveston has been the principal port of entry for Texas since its settlement. Galveston Bay is 35 or 40 miles in width, and about the same in length, being nearly circular.

Trinity river empties its waters into Galveston Bay, near the town of Anahuac, in Liberty county. Turtle, Spink's, Self's, Kettle, Milton's, and Kickapoo creeks are the principal tributaries of the Trinity from the east side; and Old river, Newman's, Cedar, and Big creeks, on the west; all in Liberty county. This county is bounded on the east by Jefferson and Jasper counties, on the south by Galveston county, west by Brazoria and Harris counties, and on the north by Houston county, and contains territory enough to make six counties of the usual size. Trinity river runs through the whole length of this county. Liberty is the seat of justice, and is situated on the east bank of the river, is a very considerable town, and is fast improving.

Liberty county is generally well timbered with oaks of all kinds, cedar, elm, ash, walnut, pecan, &c., with the exception of that part near the mouth of the river, which is mostly level, poor prairie. The bottoms are covered with heavy cane-brakes, and are subject to overflow, which renders them untillable, and dangerous to stock. Mosquitoes are very numerous here, and chills and fevers prevalent.

49

The high lands, a few miles from the river, though very heavily timbered, I consider about third rate; yet, fine cotton is grown upon them. The most of the soil is of a light grey color, and of a tough, boggy character. I do not consider this a healthy section of country, for the reasons before mentioned.

The trinity is the western boundry line of Houston and Rusk counties, and the eastern boundry line of Montgomery and Robinson counties. In Montgomery, Cummins', Harrison's, Nelson's and Bedo's creeks empty their waters into the Trinity. These creeks drain a richer region of country than that noticed in Liberty county. Much of it is prairie, and very rich, being a dark clay soil. The timbered land in these two last named counties, is generally productive, the soil being sandy, and of a dark yellow color. This is a fine cotton growing country, and some experiments have removed all doubt of its producing sugar cane to a great extent, when properly cultivated.

On the head waters of the above named creeks, many fine springs of pure, healthy water may be found. This part of the county is already thickly settled, and some fine mills and cotton gins have been built on these creeks. The bottom lands here, are subject to the same objections mentioned to those in Liberty county.

The town of Cincinnati is situated on the west bank of the Trinity, about midway the mouths of Bedo's and Nelson's creeks. This town is destined to be a large commercial city. Like her namesake, on the Ohio river in the United States, she is springing up as by magic, and judging from present appearances, there is but little doubt tbut her increase in population and improvements will be in about the same ratio that marked he growth of the latter place. The San Antonio road is the northern boundry of Montgomery county, and divides it from Robinson county.

In Houston county, Walnut, Whiterock, Barton's Negro, Hurricane, Elkhart, Catfish, and several other smaller creeks, are tributaries to the Trinity. These streams drain a diversified country, not unlike that described in Montgomery county, on the opposite side of the river, below the San Antonio road. These last named creeks empty into the Trinity above this road, and opposite to Robinson county. The town of Alabama is situated on the east bank of the Trinity, a few miles below the mouth of Hurricane creek. Parkersville is about 40 miles above, on the same side of the river, and seven miles west of Fort Houston. Both of these towns are rapidly improving, and will soon be largely populated. The latter town has only been located about 12 months. The surrounding country is fast settling by an industrious, farming community, and there are now two extensive saltworks in operation within five miles of the town. Less than two years since, there was not a house within seven miles of the spot on which the town now stands, on one side, and on the other, the nearest house was distant sixty miles.

As before mentioned, Crockett is the seat of justice of Houston county. It is on the San Antonio road, 25 miles east of Robbin's ferry. Here, the soil, timber, water, &c., are so very similar to that already described on the Sabine, Cypress, &c., that a description of it is deemed unnecessary. There are many very fine mill-streams in this county. The county on the north side of the San Antonio road, is much more desirable than that on the south side; being more healthy, better watered and more fertile.

On the head-waters of the three last named creeks, large bodies of iron ore may be found. In the country around Fort Houston, which is 35 miles from Crockett, wheat grows well, so far as has been tried. Here, there are but few prairies, and those very small. Progressing towards the northern part of this county, we leave the pine timber country, prairies become more frequent, are larger, and the land is of a better quality. The most important objection to this part of the country, is the scarcity of timber, and the inferior quality of what little there is; it being small, scrubby post oak.

ROBINSON AND RUSK COUNTIES—TRINITY COLONY, &c.

We will now notice the west side of the river, or Robinson county, which lies north of the San Antonio road. This county extends to the head waters of the Trinity, and even to the northern boundry line of Texas; a distance of 750 or 800 miles, and contains as much territory as the State of Kentucky, if not more.

To enter into a minute and intelligible description of the immense tract of country, would not only be impossible, under existing circumstances, but useless. One difficulty is, the numerous and different names given to the streams, prairies, &c., in this country; and another is, that much the largest portion of it has never been traveled over by any white man within my knowledge. I shall, therefore, expect my readers to be satisfied with a general description of that portion of this vast territory, which has come under my own observation.

A small portion of this country has been located by military and other land claimants. Much more of it would have been located, but for the opposition of the hostile Indians that infest the largest portion of it. There is but one public road in this country, and that is in the vicinity of the town of Franklin, situated about 15 miles north of the San Antonio road, and nearly 60 miles from the southeast corner of the county, or Robin's ferry.

Including the Cross Timbers, and a considerable, portion of the country below, is located the new, or what is called "Trinity Colony," which will be described in its proper place. Boggy creek empties into the Trinity five miles above Robin's Ferry. On this creek is Boggy Fort, which though much exposed to the Indians, has been sustained. Above this there are many small streams, each having almost as many different names as the number of persons that have crossed them. Tawacona, Keacheye, Elm, Grindstone, Richland, &c. These creeks, head in a prairie country, which is truly beautiful and rich. There is not a more salubrious climate in the world than this.

In speaking of a healthy section of country, I wish to be understood as excepting the river and creek bottoms, in all cases, as they, with a very few exceptions, being low and boggy, renders the country in their vicinity, unhealthy—nor do I wish to be understood as attributing to these locations, in Texas, a more unhealthy atmosphere than like causes would produce in any country. I have said I would give an *impartial* history of the country, and I am determined to redeem my pledge, if possible.

This rich and beautiful country extends from Robin's Ferry to the Cross Timbers, a distance of nearly 200 miles. Many travelers through this country, *that is,* W. and N. W. of Fort Houston, have given it as their opinion that it is the garden-spot of the world. These prairies, are in many places, covered with the Muskete grass, which is acknowledged to be the most nutricious, for stock, ever discovered.

The new colony, includes the country on the Trinity river, and on the N. E. to Red river. It also includes the Cross Timbers, and runs a considerable distance down the Trinity river. I do not know the Southern boundary of this colony, but it runs S. W. to the heights between Trinity and Brazos

52

rivers. There are immense mountains of iron ore in the country west of Fort Houston, which is richer if possible than those mentioned on the east of Fort Houston.

As before mentioned, there is much of the county of Robinson that yet remains to be located and has never been traveled over by the white man. So far, however, as I have examined that county, I have no hesitation in asserting that the largest body of good land to be found in Texas lies on the head waters of the Trinity, in this county, in the 33rd deg. N. Lat., and 21st deg. of W. long. from Washington City.

The whole northern section of Robinson county may be set down as a diversified country, to the head of the Trinity, which is in the large prairie N. W. of the Cross Timbers. The land is generally rich in the prairies, and well calculated for agriculture. The timbered lands vary in quality; there being some very rich land, and much poor; generally well watered and healthy. Much of the extreme northern part of this county which extends to Oregon Territory has never been explored.

Rush county, which borders on the Trinity for about half the length of Robinson, on the east side of the river, contains a territory very similar to that described in the latter county. Cedar Creek, and Bois d'Arc are the principal tributaries of Trinity river in Rush county. It is necessary to mention here that there are two Bois d'Arc rivers in Texas; the one just mentioned, and the one previously mentioned, which empties into Red River. They head nearly together, and take their names from the same cause, (the quantity of that timber found on them,) and might be distinguished by calling the one that empties into Red river, Northern Bois d'Arc, and the one emptying into Trinity river, Southern Bois d'Arc.

Trinity river is navigable to the mouth of Southern Bois d'Arc, and in fact a considerable distance above. The whole distance may be navigated from its mouth, may be set down at between 700 and 800 miles.

SAN JACINTO RIVER—BUFFALO BAYOU—CITY OF HOUSTON, &c., &c.

We will now return to Galveston Bay, and ascending San Jacinto river, (which comes next in order) describe the country on either side.

The San Jacinto empties into Galveston Bay, and has its head in Montgomery county, meandering its way through Harris county. Buffalo Bayou forms a junction with the San Jacinto from the west side, near the bay. It was near this place, that was fought the memorable battle of San Jacinto. On the head of this bayou stands the city of Houston, which city was located and settled in 1837, and now numbers near 10,000 inhabitants. There are now published in that city 4 or 5 interesting newspapers, and the rapid increase of business of every kind gives promise of this city's rivaling, in a few years cities of four times her age in the United States.

The country around Houston is far from prepossessing either in the quality of its soil or appearance of the face of the country. The land is generally level, poor, and boggy, growing on the higher grounds, tall pines, of excellent quality, whilst the timber in the bottoms is diversified.

Buffalo Bayou is natural canal, and is navigable as high as the city of Houston, for the largest class of steam boats, at all seasons of the year. In the year 1837, the seat of Government was located at Houston, and a most costly and magnificent capitol built there. This wass doubtless, one cause of the rapid growth of the city; though after the seat of government was removed to the city of Austin, it continued to improve as fast as it did before.

Spring Creek next empties its waters into the San Jacinto on the west side. On this creek is a fine settlement of industrious and wealthy citizens. Maj. Croft has erected a most excellent mill on this creek. It heads in a large, poor prairie, which extends nearly to the Brazos river, and south, to the Gulf. Mill creek and Lake creek come in next above, on the same side. These creeks drain a large, rich country of excellent land, which is well timbered and well watered. Lake creek heads in what is called the rotten limestone region with which the water is strongly impregnated, and thereby rendered both unpleasant and unhealthy. The land is high and rolling, and with the exception of its boggy tendency in a wet season, is well adapted to agriculture. The prairies are small and very rich, and are surrounded by the most valuable timber, such as pine, cedar, oaks of all kinds, ash, pecan, elm, &c.

Returning to the east side of San Jacinto, twenty-five miles above the city of Houston, the east and west forks of the San Jacinto have their junction. Below this point, the country is low, poor and boggy, as it is also for a considerable distance below. Above this low level country, is what is called the

54

Big Thicket, which extends nearly to Trinity river, a distance of 45 miles. We shall not attempt a description of this thicket, as there is not a man now living or dead, that is known to have explored it. In some places it is an entire and impenetrable matt of vines, briars, thorn bushes, &c, &c. Where this is not the case, cane grows so large and thick that it is also impenetrable; and the tallest trees ever seen by any person we have met with yet, (and who have seen this thicket,) are found here.

Ascending the east fork of the San Jacinto about 40 miles, we come to a thickly settled country. The farms here are in a high state of cultivation, on which are grown, cotton, corn, rye, potatoes, &c. This is in Montgomery county. The inhabitants are an industrious, moral people, who have erected several houses of religious worship, and established good schools.

The fork of the San Jacinto heads, near the town of Huntsville, which is situated 12 miles south of Cincinnati. The average distance from San Jacinto river to the Trinity is about 30 miles. This county is also rapidly settling with an industrious farming community. Towns are springing up, and stores, cotton gins, mills, &c., are numerous enough for all necessities. This region of country is not infected with the rotten lime stone spoken of on the head of Lake creek, and the water is consequently as pure, and the general health of the inhabitants is as good as that of the inhabitants of any part of the United States. Any person not acquainted wtih this section of country, and not having witnessed the scene, would be utterly astonished, could I inform them of the quantity of cotton raised and annually shipped at Cincinnati for Sabine and Galveston cities.

There are many other tributaries of the San Jacinto from this (the east) side. Sandy Creek is a beautiful stream for mills; and the land on either side is rich and well watered. The timber is also very fine. There is also a large settlement on this creek.

The high lands in all this county are boggy in wet weather; that is, the country south of the San Antonio road to the Gulf of Mexico, a distance varying from 175 to 200 miles.

The San Jacinto river is navigable for small class steamboats, a distance of 100 miles from its mouth, at all seasons of the year.

55

BRAZOS RIVER—BRAZORIA, FORT BEND, AUSTIN, WASHINGTON, MILAM AND BRAZOS COUNTIES— CITIES OF VELASCO, BRAZORIA, RICHMOND, WASHINGTON, &c. &c.

The river Brazos empties into the Gulf of Mexico, southwest of the city of Galveston, about forty miles. At the mouth of the Brazos are situated the towns of Velasco and Quintana; the former on the east, and the latter on the west side. This river runs through Brazoria, Fort Bend, and Austin counties, and is the line between Montgomery and Washington, and Washington and Brazos, and Robinson and Milam counties.

There are numberless tributaries to the Brazos on either side, many of which are unworthy of notice, although they are laid down on Hunt and Randell's map. I would here state that there are many inaccuracies in this map, though as a chart of the general face of Texas, it is tolerably correct.

Ascending the Brazos, the town of Brazoria, which is the county seat of Brazoria county, is the first town of importance. It is a fine flourshing town, and promises to be a formidable rival of her commercial sisters. The country on either side of the river, in this county, is about equally divided into bottom and high land; the latter being principally prairie, which is poor and boggy; except that portion of it which borders on the bottoms. The bottom land and the prairies for a distance of one or two miles out from these bottoms are very rich. The river and creek bottoms are very heavily timbered with live-oak of fine quality, ash, hickory, pecan, &c., &c. This county is very thickly settled and is a fine cotton growing country. Good water is very scarce here, and it is unhealthy. Columbia, a large and fast improving town, is near this river, and in this county; and is about fifteen miles from Brazoria. It was at Columbia that the first Congress met under the present form of government, (i. e.) after the adoption of the present constitution. Owensborough, and Monticello, are two small towns, also on the Brazos river and in this county, above Columbia.

Having ascended the Brazos about 80 miles, we come to Fort Bend county. Richmond is the county seat of this county, and is a flourishing place. Here, there is a paper published, and all mechanical business is profitable. The soil, timber, water, &c., &c., in this county, are so similar to that described in Brazoria county, that we pass it by without any farther comment.

Next above is Austin county, of which San Phillippe De Austin, is the county seat. It was here the Provisional Congress first met and adjourned thence to Washington, where the Declaration of Independence was signed. This county varies very little, in soil, climate, &c., from the last named.

Still ascending this river, we now come to the county of Washington. Washington City, where Congress has met for the last two sessions, by proclamation of President Houston, (he deeming Austin, the seat of Government, unsafe, from its frontier location,) is a flourishing city. It now numbers about 3,000 souls, and is surrounded by a rich tract of country, which is thickly settled by an industrious and wealthy community. The city of Washington is destined to be one of the largest and most pleasant cities in Texas. It is about 200 miles above the mouth of the Brazos. There is now published at Washington city a valuable and ably conducted paper, which is edited by the Hon. Thomas Johnson, and has a wide circulation and an extensive influence in Texas.

Mill creek, which empties into the Brazos, in Austin county 8 miles above San Phillippe De Austin, and heads in Washington county, drains a large tract of excellent country. New Years creek which also empties into the Brazos on the same side, but in Washington county, about ten miles below Washington city, also drains a fine section of country. On these two creeks are large wealthy settlements. The soil here produces well, but is difficult to cultivate on account of its tough waxy properties. Here, too, rotten limestone like that spoken of on Lake creek, is found to abound in large quantities, and as before stated, renders the water unpleasant and unhealthy.

All those counties, viz: Brazoria, Fort Bend, Austin and Washington, are thickly settled by a wealthy, moral and industrious population. The staple products of these counties are cotton, corn, rye, potatoes, &c., which are raised in abundance. Some of the farmers have tried the cultivation of sugar cane, and have succeeded admirably; which removes all doubt of its becoming, at no distant day, one of the principal products of this section of the country.

Opposite to Washington county, on the east side of the Brazos, is Montgomery county, the largest portion of which has been described. That portion of this county bordering on the Brazos is also very rich, only small portions of which abound in rotten limestone. About 35 miles east by southeast from Wash-

57

ington city, is the town of Montgomery, which is the seat of Justice of Montgomery county. This town being near the edge of the county, and consequently not well calculated for the seat of Justice, has not improved much. The land in this county, bordering on the Brazos, is not unlike that described in Washington county.

About 25 miles northwest from the town of Montgomery there is a fine blue Sulphur Spring, the waters of which is highly recommended and much used for medical purposes. I should have noticed that on the Trinity river, at the town of Carolina, also in this county, there are as many as twenty two springs of white and yellow sulphur, all within the space of half a mile. There is also a valuable spring of blue sulphur at the town of Cincinnati.

Immediately opposite the city of Washington, the Navasott river empties into the Brazos. This river is the dividing line between Montgomery and Brazos counties. Above the mouth of the Navasott, about 12 miles, Yeawa creek empties into the Brazos from the west side. This creek drains a large body of excellent country. The town of Independence is situated on this creek, and the settlement surrounding it, is said to be the most wealth ysettlement in Texas. It is called Cole's settlement.

Tenoxteland (an old Spanish Garrison,) is about 50 miles above Washington. Between these places are several creeks, and a fine country; the timber and prairie being suitably interspersed. Nashville (as well as the last named Garrison,) is in Milam county, at the mouth of Little river, ten miles above Tenoxteland. This is a very rapid stream, and drains an immense tract of rich prairie country. Fine springs are found on the tributaries of Little river, and timber is very scarce and indifferent. There are many fine mill sites on this river, and rock in abundance, handy for building. This river heads in the Colorado mountains. These mountains run nearly to the Brazos river. Basque river, some 50 miles above, also heads in the same range of mountains. The country on the west side of the Brazos, becomes very broken above the mouth of the Basque, which description of country extends to Grand Prairie.

On the east side of the Brazos, and above the mouth of the Navasott, Brazos county occupies a large territory. The Navasott, is a dull heavy running stream. On the head of this river, stood Port Parker, the capture of which the reader is already well acquainted. This fort was about 45 miles west from Fort Houston, and about 30 miles east of the Falls of Brazos. The tributaries to the Navasott are beautiful streams; there are many fine springs found on these creeks, and the land is rich.

This was my choice of all Texas; where I located and built Fort Parker, and it would be dissimulation in me to omit giving it as my opinion that the country on the Navasott is the most fertile, most healthy, and subject to fewer objections than any other part of Texas. There are some springs in this section that afford water enough to turn a mill. The timber is very large, and of an excellent quality. The rock found along these creeks, and which is abundant, is well adapted for building purposes. The range for stock is not surpassed in any country. There are many salt licks and game is plenty.

A few miles above Fort Parker, stands the remains of an Indian town called Tiwackena, and here are the Tiwackena springs. Near this place was fought the Tiwackena battle, on the 11th of July 1844, between R. M. Coleman, with a company of twenty-one men, and a band of the Tiwackena Indians numbering about 200. Coleman was defeated with the loss of one man killed, and five wounded, one whom subsequently died. In this battle, a Mr. Wallace was shot through the head and recovered from his wounds.

West of Fort Parker, the Little Brazos has its head, and runs parallel with the main Brazos at a distance of three or four miles. Between these two streams is one large bottom, twenty-five miles long, and is very rich. Little Brazos is not more than thirty-five or forty miles long, and empties into the Brazos about thirty miles above the mouth of the Navasott. There is a range of prairie commencing at Fort Parker, and running on the high ground between the Brazos and Trinity rivers, to the Cross Timbers, being, in some places, from five to six miles wide.

The Aquella river empties into the Brazos about twenty miles above the falls, and heads in the last named prairie, about twenty-five miles north of Fort Parker. The tributaries of the Aquella are much like those of the Navasott, there being many fine springs found on them, and many of them fine mill streams. The timber on these streams is also fine; being principally oak, ash, elm, walnut, pecan, &c. On the high ground there is considerable live oak, which may also be found in many places below this, on the Brazos. Near the mouth of the Aquella is the old Wako Indian town, which is a beautiful site for a town.

Above this there are many considerable streams, tributaries to the Brazos. At a very trifling expense, the Brazos river may be rendered navigable for small steamboats for a distance of 500 miles above the falls; which would be from the Gulf about 800 miles. The principal head of the Brazos is in Grand Prairie, and some of its head streams have their beginning in the Salt Plains. During a flood in the Brazos, if it is produced by heavy rains on these last named branches, the whole river is so impregnated with salt as to be very perceptible to the taste.

Aquella river is a very rapid stream, and its waters are so very clear, that the traveler cannot avoid lingering on its banks to watch the beautiful ripples made by the swift passing waters over the red pebbles, of which the bed of the river is principally composed, and witness the playful revels of the numberless perch, bass, red-horse, salmon and other fish, which may be seen in the curling eddies of this crystal stream.

The Falls of the Brazos, of which mention has been made, are about fifty miles above the city of Washington. At a very high stage of water, these falls, like those on the Ohio river, may be ascended and descended by steamboats of any capacity; but in a moderate stage of water, they are an insurmountable obstruction to navigation, the fall being six feet perpendicular, in the channel. Just above the falls is the town of Milam, which is fast improving, and when the immense and rich country above becomes settled, must be an important city.

The banks on either side of the Falls are admirably adapted for a canal, and no doubt, one day or other, a canal will be made around the Falls.

SAN BERNARD RIVER

This river empties into the Gulf of Mexico about twenty-five miles southwest of the mouth of Brazos, and has its head in a large poor prairie west of San Phillippe. In its way to the gulf, it passes through a very rich region of country, which lies in Matagorda and Brazoria counties. It is the dividing line between Fort Bend and Matagorda counties, and has its head in Colorado county. The country on this river is now densely settled, and the inhabitants grow large quantities of cotton and sugar. It is believed that there is no land in he world that produces more cotton or sugar to the acre than this, nor of a better quality. It is very heavily timbered with cypress, oak, pecan, &c. It is (or was) an almost entire cane brake, from the San

60

Bernard to a creek called Old Cany. Lenville creek is a tributary of the Cany, and heads near the Colorado. The country on either side of the San Bernard to the Brazos on the north, and the Colorado on the south, is not surpassed in fertility by any county in the United States.

Good water is not to be found here, and this region of country is decidedly unhealthy. Cotton grows here to an incredible height, as also does sugar cane; which latter is said to ripen two feet higher than it does in Louisiana.

COLORADO RIVER—MATAGORDA BAY—MATAGORDA, COLORADO, FAYETTE, BASTROP, AND BEXAR COUNTIES—CITIES OF MATAGORDA, COLUMBUS, LAGRANGE, COLORADO, BASTROP AND AUSTIN.

The Colorado river has its head in Grand Prairie, and meanders, as it best can find its way, through a high mountainous country for a distance of 300 miles at least, before it reaches a rolling country, which commences in Fayette county, and passing on pours its waters into Matagorda bay on the Gulf of Mexico. It runs through Matagorda county. The city of Matagorda is at the mouth of the river on the east bank, is a beautiful city and numbers about 2,000 inhabitants. The land in Matagorda county is so very similar to that just described on San Bernard river, that I shall pass it by without further notice. I would mention, however, the Matagorda bay is as notorious for the number and size of the mosquitoes bred in its waters as it is for the quantity of its oysters.

Jennings' and Jones' creeks empty into the Colorado in this county on the west side. Ascending this river, we next come to Colorado county, through which it passes nearly centrally. Columbus, the county seat of Colorado county, is a fine flourishing place, and is situated on the west bank of the river. There are no streams of importance tributary to the Colorado in this county. Near the river the land is generally fertile; but much the largest portion of this county is poor, particularly that on the east side of the river. There is no good water in either of these last named counties.

Fayette county next comes in order, as we ascend the Colorado. Lagrange is the seat of justice. It is on the east bank of the river, and is fast improving. The land is much better in this, than in the two last named counties; being more rolling and

61

better watered. Ruterville is a flourishing little town, five miles from Lagrange, and has a well regulated college established in it.

I have neglected to mention, that in all the thickly settled portions of Texas, good schools have been established, and houses of religious worship have been built; and the morals of the inhabitants are not surpassed by that of any community in the world.

The city of Colorado is on the west bank of the river, a few miles above the town of Lagrange. Buckner's creek empties its waters into Colorado river nearly opposite the latter place; and Cummins' creek, which heads in this county, also empties into the Colorado, near Columbus.

The face of the country, and quality of the soil, water and timber, is very different in this county from that in Matagorda and Colorado counties. Springs are numerous, and the land being high and rolling, it is much more healthy. This county is densely settled.

Next above comes Bastrop county, and the mountainous country now commences. Berlison, Bastrop, and the city of Austin are on the N. E. side of the river, all in Bastrop county. The former is about 14 miles below the town of Bastrop, and Gen. E. Burlison is the proprietor. The country around this place is thickly settled, and the land rich and the climate healthy.

Bastrop is about 10 miles below the mouth of Welburger's creek, and about 35 miles below the city of Austin. It is a flourishing town, and has an excellent steam grist and saw mill, several cotton gins, stores, taverns, and nearly all the different branches of mechanical business is carried on. Business of every kind appear prosperous, and Bastrop is destined, beyond a doubt, to be a considerable place of business. It now numbers nearly 3,000 inhabitants.

The city of Austin, in this county, and on the same side of the Colorado, is the seat of Government of Texas. It is near the Colorado mountains, and is, perhaps, as healthy a position as any in the world. Its being so near the frontier, and in the neighborhood of the Comanche Indians, prevents it from improving very fast; but there is no doubt but it will be a large city so soon as these hindrances to its growth are removed. There is a very valuable paper published here at this time, which is edited by S. Whiting, Esq.

Walnut creek empties into the Colorado from the west side, a few miles below Bastrop. The town of Comanche is on this

62

side of the river just below Onion creek. About 25 miles above Bastrop, on the west side of the river, there are many tributaries to the Colorado; but being small, we will pass them without further notice. The country in this county is beautiful beyond description. This is the first point in our description of Texas that we meet with the mountains. Below the city of Austin the county is tolerably thickly settled; but after passing a few miles above, there are no settlements at all.

Ascending the Colorado, above Austin, the traveler meets with an entirely different country from any that has been described. Traveling on any of the rivers previously noticed, or below this, on the Colorado, a person sitting on the hurricane deck of a steamboat, may (where the timber does not intervene,) see over the face of the country, in some places, a distance of two or three miles; but now ascending the Colorado, he comes to perpendicular mountains of immense height.

This river has never been navigated, and it is doubtful whether it ever will be, for the reasons that it is very rapid and very rocky, and also very crooked. In many places it falls as much as five or six feet in a distance of 30 or 40 yards. There is a very large raft near its mouth, which might be removed at a trifling expense, and then it might be navigable as high, perhaps, as Columbus, in Colorado county. Those, however, who are well acquainted with this river, and better acquainted with navigation than I am, think it will never be navigated with any degree of success.

As has been before stated, the city of Austin is near the foot of a range of abrupt mountains on the east bank of the river. These rugged mountains close in entirely to the bed of the river in many places, thereby rendering them almost impassable. North of this, however, there is an extensive tract of desirable country. There are many beautiful tributaries in this country above the mountains. Those coming in from the right hand, or east side of this river, have their heads in the Grand Prairie, and those on the left hand, or west side, head in the table lands northwest of this range of mountains. Pierdenales river runs through a mountainous country, and empties into the Colorado in these mountains.

Near the head of this river is what is called the "Enchanted Rock." Much has been said about this rock. It stands entirely to itself, and is about 200 feet high. (I must state, however, that I know nothing of this singular rock myself, having never been to it, and only state what those have told me, in whom I have confidence; leaving the reader to draw his own inference and come to his own conclusions as to the truth or falsity of the tale.) It is said to be accessible only on one side, and that by a natural flight of stairs winding around it to the top. It is said that when a person approaches this rock, a singular light surrounds him, the source of which cannot be discovered. It is also said that when on this rock he is in involuntary motion, whilst his ears continually saluted by strange sounds, as if many persons were talking in different languages around him.

I am no believer in ghosts, hob-goblins or enchantments, and nothing has induced me to give credit to any thing I have heard about this "Enchanted Rock," but the highly creditable source of my information. If all is true that I have heard about it, when visited by the learned and curious, it will afford a wide field for mysterious speculation.

San Saba river also heads in this range of mountains on the west side of the Colorado, into which it empties its waters. On the head waters of the San Saba there is much beautiful country, which abounds in fine springs and large creeks. On the waters of this river are the celebrated San Saba mines, which are thought to be the richest and most extensive silver mines in the world. They have been extensively worked, but by whom I know not; but from appearances, there have been thousands of pounds of silver procured here; and the millions that I believe yet remain are incalculable. The ore is very rich, and I believe, entirely inexhaustible, and very accessible. The day is not far distant, when these and other valuable silver mines in Texas will be extensively and profitably worked. This range of mineral extends in an easterly direction. I have discovered what I believe to be this vein, at least 500 miles from the above named place; and others are said to have discovered it in other places. In some places in this region there are many appearances of gold.

These mines are in the Comanche range, and the warlike disposition and deadly hostility of these Indians to the Texans, has prevented them from taking advantage of the immense wealth here available; but this obstacle will not, I think, exist much longer; for if there is not a treaty effected with these Indians very soon, there will be such a company raised for the purpose of working these mines, as to bid defiance to all opposition from that quarter.

64

There is an old trail leading from the city of San Antonio across the heads of the Piedernales, San Saba, Rio Colorado de Texas, Rio Aquilas, Rio Pisapejenova, Rio Pasigona, &c., &c., to Santa Fe. This trace leads through the table lands which are the heights between, and divide the waters of the Colorado and Rio Grande. These table lands are known to but few. I have traveled over the greater part of them, and should have went farther, but for the difficulty of traveling. As far as I have been into this table land country, (which I am told extends to the Rio Grande,) there is such a similarity in it, that but few remarks will suffice.

These table lands are a great curiosity. The traveler will think himself on an interminable plain, but after progressing some two or three miles, he will come to an abrupt perpendicular rocky cleft, some 10, 20 and others 50 feet high, which he finds great difficulty in ascending. After having gained the top, he finds himself on another apparently interminable plain, but pursuing his journey, he soon comes to another obstruction, so like the one just surmounted, that he is almost made to doubt whether it is not the same. At other times he comes to these projections and has to descend them, which he sometimes finds more difficult than to ascend.

These levels are very rich, having a dark loam soil. The timber is objectionable for its inferior quality, and is very scarce. It is principally post oak, muskite, some little ash, elm, and pecan. Spanish, persimmon, buckeye and mulberry. There is not to be found, I am sure, in any part of the world, purer water; nor do I believe there is a spot on the inhabitable globe better calculated to insure good health and long life. Whilst there, I did not see a single mosquito, tick or fly of any description. The atmosphere here is so pure, that I have killed buffaloes and the whole carcase would become dry and firm, if hung up, before it would spoil.

If this region of country was not infested by hostile Indians, it would be very soon settled; and when once settled and cultivated by civilized man, it will approximate to an earthly paradise, as nearly as man could wish. I have no correct idea of the extent of this table land country, but have no doubt that it is as large at the State of Indiana. These table lands lie about the center of Bexar county, north of the Colorado range of mountains.

To undertake to describe all the tributaries to the Colorado, would swell this volume far beyond the limits I have prescribed to it. Nor is it necessary, for they are so very similar, that a description of one answers very well for all adjacent to it. Besides this, although I have traveled over this vast region of country as much, perhaps, as any other living man, there is much of it that I have never yet seen, and in this history I have determined to describe that country only which has come under my own observation. Others have described many parts of Texas from second hand information, and I have found it will not do, if the author wishes to do justice either to the country or to his readers.

Trespalacios, a small Bayou that empties into Trespalacios Bay, which runs into Matagorda Bay. The town of Tide Haven is on the west bank of this bayou, some 15 miles from the bay. Caranchua bayou, 12 miles west, also empties into the Matagorda bay. Mustang's Navodad, and Labaca (or Cow) creeks form a junction a few miles below the town of Texana, which is the county seat of Jackson county, and empty into Labaca bay, which also runs into Matagorda bay. The last named creek, (i. e,) Labaca, is the western line of this county, dividing it from Victoria county.

In Jackson county, as in all the counties on the coast, the lands bordering immediately on the coast, and tributary streams, are very rich, while the high ground is poor boggy prairie. This is a fine section of country for raising stock, the range being most excellent. There are few fine springs in this county.

GUADALOUPE OR WAR LOOPE RIVER — ESPIREIN SANTA BAY—SAN ANTONIO RIVER — REFUGIO, VICTORIA—GOLIAD AND GONZALES COUNTIES— CITIES OF VICTORIA, GONZALES, AND SAN ANTONIO.

The rivers Guadaloupe and San Antonio, form a junction about 15 miles from Victoria city, and after passing a distance of 14 or 15 miles form Espirein Santa bay. The county of Victoria is on the east, and the county of Refugio, on the west of Gaudaloupe river, it being the dividing line.

The city of Victoria is the county seat of Victoria county, is a fine flourishing place, numbering near 4,000 inhabitants; and although it is much exposed to the hostile Indians, it has sustained itself, and is fast improving. This city stands immediately on the east bank of the river Gaudaloupe, and is surrounded by a rich prairie.

The city of Refugio is the seat of justice of Refugio county and stands on the east bank of the little river Copano, which forms Copano bay. The town of Copano is on the head of this bay, and like Refugio, has not improved much, on account of their exposure to Indian depredations. When this obstacle is removed both these places will rise to distinction.

There are three objections to these counties, viz: the timber, water and soil. There is little timber in these counties except what is found on the water courses, and that not only scarce, but very indifferent. Some little post oak is sometimes found on the high lands; elm, ash, pecan, &c., in the bottoms. Good water is also very scarce, and can only be obtained by digging wells. The soil is generally of a tough clay, sticky nature, and it is difficult and even hazardous to travel over it at certain seasons of the year, and cannot be cultivated in a wet season, owing to its waxy quality. In some places, however, a sandy soil is found, which like some of the sticky land produces well in a dry season.

Notwithstanding these objections, these counties are fast being populated by an industrious, enterpising people, who raise fine crops of cotton, corn, &c. and any number of mules, horses, cattle and hogs.

There are many other streams tributary to the bays and rivers, in these two counties, as Carcitas, Union and Chocolate bayous emptying into Labaca bay, in Victoria county; and Coloto river emptying into the Gaudalope, in the same county, whilst in Refugio county are Melon, Aransas and Chiltipin bayous emptying into Copano bay.

The county of Goliad lies next above Refugio through which the river San Antonio passes. Goliad is the seat of justice, and is situated on the west bank of this river, near the dividing line between these counties. Here was fought the battle between the advance guard of Santa Anna's army, and the troops under Col. Fannin. (This battle is noted under the head of "The Texas War.")

Gonzales county lies next above this, through which the Gaudaloupe passes. Gonzales is the name of the seat of Justice of this county. It is situated on the east bank of the Gaudeloupe river, and is a flourishing town. The river St. Marcos empties into the Gaudaloupe just above Gonzales. About 25 miles above

67

this place, on the Gaudaloupe, is situated the flourishing town of Sequin. This town was laid in ashes by Santa Anna, on his march into Texas; but it has been rebuilt, and is now fast improving.

There are many tributaries to the Gaudalope in this county. The land in this county is of a much better quality than that in the last mentioned counties. Good water is plenty, but timber is scarce and generally very inferior, being post and red oaks, ash, elm, and Pecan, some large cotton wood and white oak. Muskite timber is found in abundance in some places in this county; and where this grows, Muskie grass is also found.

In this as well as many other parts of Texas, especially Western Texas, the tough, sticky soil, before noticed abounds. During a long drough, this sticky clay land will become very hard and burst open, leaving chasms sometimes 20 feet deep, and sometimes so wide that cattle and horses fall into them, making it not only unpleasant but unsafe to ride through the woods, as the grass grows very high, and falling over these chasms, conceals them from view. When it rains these cracks close up and leave the earth very uneven, forming what are called : :hog-wallows." There are great numbers of poisonous snakes in every part of Texas, but this is more infested with rattle snakes than other parts of the country.

The St. Marcos and Gaudaloupe rivers head in the Colorado mountains. In the forks of these rivers there is a bank of ising-glass which is supposed to be the largest known of in any part of the world. It is thought that there is mineral in that county.

West of this county lies San Antonio county through which runs the San Antonio river. This river has its head in the Colorado mountains. The city of San Antonio de Bexar lies on this river. This is the place called the "*Alamo*," where so many hard battles have been fought, and where fell the brave Crockert, Travis, Bowie and their brave followers. It was here the Col. B. Milam, with about 180 men, attacked Gen. Cass, with an army of about 2,100 men, who were strongly garrisoned, and after a continued bombardment of several weeks make him surrender.

There are numerous tributaries to the San Antonio on either side in Goliad county; a few miles above the northern line of which county, this river is formed by the junction of Medina and Cibola rivers. On the former, there is much cypress timber of a superior quality which is hauled to the city of San Antonio,

68

a distance of 20 miles, and used for building purposes. The greater portion of this county, that is the inhabited portions of it, is very much like the land described in Gonzales. The timber is more indifferent and scarce, and the range better. The water near the mountains is not surpassed in quality by any in the world; but as we descend the river, springs become scarce, and the water not so good.

There is an abundance of the "hog wallow prairie" in this region. After passing the mountains, which are narrow here, the table land before described is found.

I expect there is as much territory in this, San Antonio or Bexar county, as is in the State of Tennessee and Kentucky, much the largest portion of which has never been explored, or even seen by any white man, within my knowledge, and of course only a very partial description can be expected. This fact is established, however, beyond a doubt, that the most healthy country known on the American continent is to be found in this region. This county is about equally divided into mountainous, rolling hilly and level land.

These mountains offer greater inducements to those who wish to live a hermit's life, than any place I ever saw. Here far from the range of man, in the most salubrious climate, breathing the most healthful atmosphere, drinking the purest water, and tilling the most fertile soil in the world, he could live alike unknowing and unknown, free from the strife of this busy world.

This county extends west to the Rio Grande, north to the northern boundary of Texas, and is bounded on the south by San Patricio county, and is about 350 miles in width, and 800 in length, including the Santa Fee country. I should have stated that in many other parts of Texas, as in this county, the greatest variety and most beautiful flowers I ever saw, surpassing the richest pleasure garden, grow on the prairies, as far as the imagination can conceive.

To enter into a description of all the different herbs, bushes, &c., found growing on these prairies, would occupy too much space. There are five or six different kinds of prickly pear found here—some growing like vines, and running over the bushes, which are covered with thorns. There are many kinds of wild fruit found here that I never saw any where else, some of which are very delicious. The vast region of country presents a wide field for the naturalist and the geologist.

CORPUS CHRISTI BAY—LAGUNA DEL MADRE LAKE— NUECES RIVER—SAN PATRICIO COUNTY.

Nuces river empties its waters into Corpus Christi bay, which, with other tributaries from Lake Laguna Del Madre, This river runs through the northeast corner of San Patricio county, and divides this from Refugio county. The soil, timber, &c., of San Patricio, differs so little from that already described in other counties bordering on the coast, that I shall refer the reader to a description of them, and ask him to apply it to this.

There are now no settlements in this county, never were but few, and those have long since been deserted. San Patricio county borders on the Gulf from Corpus Christi bay, to the mouth of the Rio Grande, and thence runs up this river to the town of Laredo, where San Antonio de Bexar county commences, and contains as much territory as the State of Indiana.

There is a great salt lake in this county, differing very little from those described by Mrs. Plummer in her narrative. The quantity of salt annually taken away from this lake is incalculable, as it forms as fast as it is removed.

I have traveled but little through this county, and have given a description of no country second handed. I must refer my readers to other writers for a more minute description of it.

I have been to the Rio Grande at several different points, and have found on its banks, and for a considerable distance out, boggy, marshy country, by no means prepossessing. I also found timber scarce, though there is a very large body of timbered land below the road leading from San Antonio to the interior of Mexico, which is said to be very rich.

The Rio Grande is the most turbulent stream for its size I ever saw. Although as wide as the Mississippi in some places, and wider in others, its current is much more rapid, I should think that a boat floating with the tide on the Rio Grande, would go a distance of two miles in the same time it would go one on the Mississippi. For this reason, I think it will never be profitably navigated. It is also very crooked, running to every point of the compass, in some places, in a distance of twenty miles.

The counties of San Patricio, Refugio, San Antonio, Goliad, Victoria, Jackson, and Gonzales, have suffered more from marauding parties of Mexicans and Indians, than all the balance of Texas, they being the most southwestern counties. They have been entirely depopulated several times, and some of them will,

70

perhaps, never be permanently re-settled until Mexico acknowledges the independence of Texas, and a final treaty of peace is declared. Thus has a great part of Texas been kept an entire wilderness, and much of it not even explored.

I now close this part of the geographical description of this valuable and interesting country. The reader will observe that I commenced with the extreme northeastern part of Texas, bordering on the United States, and progressed regularly to the southwestern part, bordering on Mexico; Red River being the line from whence I started, and the Rio Grande the line where I stopped. It will also be observed that I have taken the rivers as they came in rotation, and ascending them to their heads, or the northern boundary of Texas, have given such a description of the intervening country as would be interesting to the reader, or my space allow.

I shall now make a brief general view of the country, pointing out its advantages and its disadvantages; and then pass on to a brief history of the War, with which I shall close my portion of this volume.

GENERAL VIEW OF TEXAS

The face of Texas may be divided into four classes, viz: level, rolling, hilly and mountainous.

1st. The level class is that portion bordering on the Gulf of Mexico, which extends from the mouth of Sabine river to the mouth of Rio Grande, a distance of 550 or 600 miles coast wise, and varying in width from 40 to 80 miles. For a distance of a half to three miles from the coast, the land is richer, higher and dryer, with few exceptions, than it is farther out. After this high land, just on the coast, there is a continued marsh, varying from one to ten miles in width, the whole length of the coast, with a few exceptions. Along this extensive marshy strip are innumerable ponds, lakes, bays, &c., in which are found fish and fowl of nearly every kind, such as salmon, red-fish, porpoise, shark, mullet, sea-turtle, oysters, crabs, shrimps, lobsters, &c., &c., which are easily taken. Of wild fowl, there are swan, pelicans, geese, ducks of many kinds, sea-gulls, &c., &c. Egg Island, a few leagues from Matagorda, takes its name from the great number of eggs that may be found on it in the spring, which are of many sizes and colors.

Along the coast it is generally shoal water, and at low tide is

71

a sand bar for miles. Many wrecks of vessels and boats, and even very large trees are driven upon this coast by the sea surf, which flows in very strong. Large poplar trees are often washed ashore on this coast, especially at and near Sabine city, which must have come down the Mississippi river.

The counties bordering on the coast, beginning at the mouth of the Rio Grande are San Patricio, Refugio, Victoria, Jackson, Matagorda, Brazoria, Galveston, Harris, Liberty, and Jefferson. Galveston includes Galveston island. All along the coast, and especially near the sea marshes, musquitoes are plenty, and the climate unhealthy. Back of this marsh, extending to the rolling land, are generally flat, boggy prairies, except the creek and river bottoms.

The staple products of this region of country is cotton, though I think this will not be the case long, as the growing of sugar cane is fast taking its place already. I am of opinion that the growing of cotton will be confined to the second and third regions of the country, and that this coast region will grow sugar cane, rice, &c. Some are thinking of turning their attention to the growing of coffee, in the coast country; but I cannot speak positively as to what success will attend it, but I have no doubt it will be good.

Several orange orchards have been planted along the coast, which, it is thought, will produce as well as any on the Island of Cuba. Olive trees are also planted, and are growing well.

2nd. The rolling country extends from the above described level country, back to the hilly country, to, or within the vicinity of the San Antonio road, which leads from Nacogdoches, bearing in a southwesterly direction to San Antonio, and thence to the interior of Mexico. The following counties may be said to embrace the rolling country. Beginning at Sabine river and progressing southwestward, they are a part of Jasper, all of Liberty, north part of Harris, south part of Montgomery, all of Fort Bend, south part of Austin, south part of Colorado, south part of Gonzales, north part of San Patricia, and south part of San Antonio de Bexar.

This region of country may be divided into three classes: 1st. From the Sabine to the river San Jacinto. This range of country is heavily timbered and tolerably well watered, is well adapted for agriculture, and is densely settled. The principal products of this part of the country are cotton, corn, rye, potatoes, &c. Fruit of nearly every kind is cultivated with ease, and there are many orchards of fine fruit in this section.

2nd. This region of country lying between the San Jacinto and Brazos rivers, is well watered, small prairies surrounded by good timber, and has a rather better soil than that just described. It is more densely settled, and, in addition to the productions named above, sugar cane is beginning to be cultivated to some extent.

3rd. We now pass to the western division of this country lying between the Brazos and Rio Grande. Prairies now become more frequent, and are of an inferior quality; being mostly the hog-wallow prairies, previously spoken of; good water and good timber are both scarce. Many are of opinion that this description of prairie is more productive than the dry sandy-soil prairie, but I am of opinion that this is not the fact.

All this region of country, here classed as rolling I think is unhealthy, for this reason: During the spring, summer and fall seasons of the year, the southern gales from the Gulf passing over this level land, and the stagnant marshes, lakes, ponds, bays, and boggy lands, are impregnated with the unhealthy effluvia arising from their surface, and the decomposed vegetation about them. As an evidence of this, mosquitoes are almost as thick here in many places, as they are on the coast; they having been blown out by this breeze.

3rd. We next come to hilly country, which is all of that lying north of the rolling country, and south of the mountains, and running parallel with the two first described, from the Sabine to the Rio Grande. We will divide this into two classes: first, that part lying east of the Brazos, and extending to Grand Prairie, including Trinity Colony, and the Cherokee country; and secondly, all west of the Brazos to the Rio Grande, and extending from the rolling country to the Colorado mountians.

This region of country, east of the Brazos, I think the best part of Texas. I would remark that though it is called hilly, there is very little, if any of it that is too rolling for cultivation. It is generally a high, healthy, well watered and well timbered country. The timbered and prairie land is suitably interspersed, and of a rich productive quality. Mill streams are numerous and the range for stock is fine. Except in the mountain region of country that is now under consideration, is the only part of Texas where stone suitable for building is to be found. This region of country, is free from mosquitoes, though ticks are numerous. Except in very peculiar situations, such a thing as chills and fevers are seldom heard of. This region of Texas is settling very fast, though it is not so densly settled as the second class, but it is increasing in population now, faster than the last mentioned class. Many persons are annually moving from this second class to the third class, or hilly country, now under consideration.

The product of this third region of country is much the same as that in the second, with the exception of sugar cane, which is not often attempted to be cultivated. This region reaches into the buffalo range, and game of every description is more plentiful here than in the first described regions.

I have remarked that this region of country is not as thickly settled; excepting a part of the counties of Fannin, and all of Lamar, and Red River, which border on Red river, part of Harrison, bordering on the State of Louisiana, all of Shelby, Sabine and part of Jasper, lying on Sabine river; all San Augustine, greater part of Nacogdoches and parts of Montgomery, Robinson and Brazos, which are thickly settled.

Emigrants are pouring into Texas every day, by hundreds, the most of whom are settling in the section of the country now under notice. It is truly astonishing to see the improvements going on in the above counties. Mills, propelled by water, steam, horses, &c., are almost daily being built; and cotton gins, &c., &c. Many fine family mansions already add to the beauty of the country and comfort of the owners; and the villages and towns springing up—the good schools established, and the houses of religious worship built, all give evidence of the rapid strides of this flourishing young republic to prosperity and distinction. In short, the whole country appears alive to improvement; and it is only necessary that the political affairs of the country should once be properly adjusted, confidence established, and in a few years, a more prosperous, happy and virtuous people cannot be found in the world, than Texas will boast.

It is, perhaps, proper to mention here, that it is the prevalent opinion in Texas, that the seat of Government will finally be located on the Brazos, or in the section of country which lies east of the Brazos.

We will now cross the Brazos, and in this same range the face of the country will be found entirely different from that just described on the east side of this river. Here again commences the tough, sticky soil before mentioned. The prairies are large, and timber scarce; and with the exception of that portion of it which is a part of and adjacent to the Colorado mountains, the water is very indifferent.

In some places on the Little and Colorado rivers, there is much cedar of a very fine quality, particularly on the latter, above Bastrop. A part of this county is densely settled, as also are parts of Washington, Milam, Brazos, Fayette and Gonzales.

Many are of opinion that this part of Texas, in point of soil and climate, is superior to that described, in this range, east of the Brazos; but I think differently.

All men are liable to think their own section of country the most desirable; and it is as necessary that we should differ in tastes and opinions, as that we should differ in our features. Before I became interested in the prosperity of any particular part of Texas, I examined and carefully considered the properties, advantages and disadvantages of the different portions of it coming under my observation, and I then formed the same opinions I now entertain of it, and that I have here given. I may err in some immaterial points, but if I know myself, I am not influenced by prejudice.

4th. The mountainous country now claims notice; and as I have already given a description of the greatest part of them, I scarcely know where to begin.

There are few mountains in Texas, east of the Brazos river, and but few from this to the Colorado. West of the Colorado running in an almost direct westerly direction are the Colorado mountains.

Northwest of this range of mountains are the rich table lands previously described. There are in these mountains many fertile valleys, which will make the most healthy residences in the world. As before mentioned, there are many valuable mines in these mountains, which will, at no distant day, be very profitably worked. This range of mountains continues in a westerly direction until they cross the Rio Grande, and from thence they take the name of Rocky mountains, which divide Texas and the United States from the Californias and Oregon Territory.

REMARKS

Having concluded this brief geographical history of Texas, I would remark that, as many persons have performed the same duty, it seems that I should, in justice to myself, and those who have written before me, conclude with a few explanatory remarks.

In the first place, it will be observed that I have avoided, as far as possible, making sweeping declarations. I have endeavored to do entire justice to Texas, in describing its soil, climate, &c., whilst at the same time I have studiously avoided saying any thing calculated to mislead those into whose hands this little volume may fall, who now have determined, or may hereafter conclude to emigrate to that country.

It appears to me that many persons, in giving a description of a new country, are either ignorant of, or grossly callous to the injuries they may inflict upon persons who are but little able to bear them. Our location and the diversity of our pecuniary situations, materially renders us an emigrating people. As the older settled countries become populated, and large bodies of lands are concentrated into the hands of those who are more fortunate or more industrious and economical, the overplus, who are, generally speaking, poor men, are compelled to seek new homes in a new country; whilst others are influenced to do so with the view of improving their fortunes.

Some historians, appear, when they visit a new country to look at the bright side of every thing; their information is generally second-hand, and procured from persons who are prejudiced in favor of the country, or whose interest it is that it should be speedily settled. These descriptions are, with few exceptions, one sided, and calculated to deceive the reader.

I have read several descriptions of Texas, and in one sense, they are correct, whilst in another they are incorrect. I will here explain my meaning by a comparison. There grows in parts of Texas a kind of a nut, which is beautiful in appearance, and very rich and most delicious to the taste, but is very poisonous. Suppose I were to hand a number of these nuts to a friend, and say, "here are some sweet delicious nuts," and say no more; and he were to eat them, as he certainly would, and should die, would I not be held responsible for his death, both by law and justice? I certainly would. So, also, should I feel myself equally censurable, if, in giving a description of Texas, either by request or voluntarily, I should tell all that was good about it, and leave untold its bad qualities.

I flatter myself in the foregoing pages I have avoided this great error of other writers; whilst at the same time I have detracted nothing from the high character of Texas for fertility of soil and salubrity of climate. When I say that there is not a country within my knowledge of the same extent of territory as that of Texas, that has as much rich soil—that has a more general healthy atmosphere—that is blessed with better water—that has more beautiful lakes or richer landscapes—that has a more extensive range for stock—or that surpasses her in commercial, agricultural, or manufacturing advantages, I speak truly. But I can, with equal truth, say, that within my knowledge, there is not a country of the same extent that has more poor land; that has a greater number of local causes of disease—that has a larger portion of it that is without good water—that has more unseemly and disagreeable swamps and ponds, or that has more snakes, mosquitoes, ticks and flies than Texas. Having been thus candid in my description, I feel confident that I shall deceive no one. For my own part I am perfectly satisfied with it, and would not exchange situations with any man living. All my earthly interests lie in Texas, and my own prosperity is inseparably connected with the prosperity of that country; which finally depends upon its speedy settlement and improvement. Yet, as much as I desire that, and as firmly convinced as I am, that I have met with many persons in the United States whose situations would be much improved were they to go to Texas, in this description of it I have endeavored to place myself beyond the censure of those who may emigrate to that country, by describing it as it is.

There are many improper impressions entertained by the citizens of the United States, with regard to the morality of the citizens of Texas. The opinion appears to prevail here, that they are immoral, uneducated and intemperate people; and some more ignorant, and therefore less culpable than others, are pleased to denounce the citizens of Texas as a band of outlaws. I have not unfrequently had my feelings hurt by hearing our citizens denounced with such opprobrious epithets as outlaws, thieves, robbers, &c.; and have often been prevented from resenting it in a proper manner, by the insignificance, or pitiable

77

ignorance of those who used them. When I say insignificance, I mean those who are a disgarce to themselves, and a nuisance in community; and by the ignorant, I mean those with whom nature has dealt sparingly in bestowing her best gift to man— *common sense*—for none others would thus slander a people of whom they are ignorant. But what am I doing? I sincerely beg pardon of the high-minded, intelligent and noble-souled citizens of my adopted country for this uncalled for defence of their character; and I hope my readers will excuse my inadvertence in stooping to notice such filth.

Of the people of Texas I can say what all who are acquainted with the character of its citizens will bear me witness in, viz: that they are, taken as a mass, as intelligent, moral and temperate a people as is found in any country in the world. True, as in all countries, there are many intemperate and unworthy citizens in Texas, but no more not even as many, according to the population, as are found in other countries.

There is scarcely a town, or thickly settled neighborhood in Texas, that there is not an organized church and a temperance society established. Good schools are established in every neighborhood of sufficient size to support one; and several flourishing colleges are in successful operation in the principal cities and towns. In these places literary societies of high standing are in existence, and the arts and sciences are liberally patronized.

THE TEXAS WARS

There is perhaps no country of the same age, that has suffered more from the calamities of war than has this young republic. Long before Mexico attempted to rivet the chains of despotism upon her citizens, they were continually harrassed by the hostile bands of Indians within her borders. The encroachments of the Indians, however, were confined to that part of the country West of the Brazos, until the beginning of the year 1836, or until the commencement of the war between Texas and Mexico; when they, aided and abetted by the Mexicans, extended their depredations east of the Brazos river.

Until February 1835, the Indians labored under the impressions, that the Americans residing west of the Brazos, in the Colorado country, were an entirely different race from those residing east of the Brazos, and would make war upon those on the Colorado, whilst they would treat with and were friendly to those residing on the east of the Brazos. In February 1835, there was a treaty held with 12 of the principal chiefs of the hostile Indians, by Maj. Sterling C. Robertson, Maj. J. G. W. Pierson, and myself, on the part of Texas, at which we convinced them that they had been in error, and they stipulated to act peacefully towards the western settlers in future. These treaty stipulations were faithfully complied with until 1836, when hostilities were recommenced, through the influences above mentioned.

The Mexican government had a line of garrisons, stationed as follows: One at Velasco, one at Nacogdoches, under the command of Cols. Pedros and Bean, one at Anahuac, under Col. Bradburn, (who was an American, and I think a Kentuckian by birth,) and one at Tenoxteland. The regular troops stationed at these garrisons were continually committing depradations upon the civil citizens in their neighborhoods, by stealing their poultry, hogs, and in short every thing they needed at their garrisons. In addition to this annoyance, the officers were very overbearing and cruel to the citizens, with which they forebore until forbearance ceased to be a virtue.

Col. Bradburn, commanding the garrison at Anahuac, was particulatly tyranical, and in the spring of 1831, a Col. Jack, a private citizen, happened to offer some trifling insult to Col. Bradburn, who had him arrested and imprisoned, where he was most barbarously treated. This aroused the citizens to a point they could no longer endure, and having procured an old field-piece, (one perhaps that had been in the service of La Fitte, and was picked up on the coast,) they fitted it upon a pair of cart wheels, and having gathered a promiscuous company, some 200 or 300 strong, marched down to Anahuac. About 24 hours before they reached the garrison, Col. Bradburn had started a schooner, with Col. Jack to Mexico, to stand his trial, for the trifling insult offered him. The Mexican laws were such, that the least insult offered one of her military officers was considered treason, and punished by death.

Providence however interfered in this case; as a strong head-wind set in soon after the vessel started, which increased to a heavy gale, and in spite of the efforts of the crew, she was driven back into the bay, just as the little army reached the place. A hard fought battle now ensued, in which the garrison was defeated, and Col. Jack released. Col. Bradburn, and his surviving troops were permitted to live, provided they would immediately leave the country, which they did.

A part of this little army returned to their families, whilst the remainder, which was recruited by boys, (some of whom were not more than 14 years of age,) marched on to attack the garrison at Velasco, at the mouth of Brazos river. This garrison was also defeated, and the troops stationed there were also required to leave the country, which they did. This little army now disbanded and returned to their homes.

This chastisement of the insolence and dishonesty of the Mexicans caused the troops and officers still remaining in the country, to alter their course of conduct; and things went on tolerably well until 1833, when the troops stationed at Nacogdoches, presuming upon their strength, (there being stationed there, at that time, a regiment of dragoons,) began again to take unwarranted privileges, and to treat the American citizens tyranically. This again aroused the blood of the Texans, and a force was soon raised to drive the Mexicans from the country. The Texans fortified themselves in a large stone house within gun shot of the garrison, and it was two or three days before the Mexican troops were forced to evacuate the place. After the loss of several men, they, under the cover of night, left the garrison, but were pursued and overtaken at Angalana river, where many of them were killed, the Texans not losing a single man. All the Mexican garrisons in Texas were now deserted, and all went on amicably until 1835.

For a year or two previous to this time a revolution had been going on in Mexico, in which Texas took no part; but this revolution having been brought on by Santa Anna, for the purpose, as he and his friends declared, of establishing a more republican form of government, the Texans were in favor of his success. He did succeed; and instead of a republican form of Government, a despotic government was established, and he had himself declared Dictator for life. Now enthroned in power, influenced and dictated to by the Priesthood of Mexico, he set about removing all obstacles to his continuance in power; the most formidable of which was the rifles of the people. It was therefore necessary that they should be disarmed, and that strong standing armies should be kept up to keep them so. In addition to this, heavy and insupportable taxes were levied to support these standing armies, and church tythes were also levied to support her indolent priesthood.

Texas now despatched a special minister (Gen. Stephen F. Austin,) to remonstrate against these grievances, who was seized and imprisoned; and Gen. Coss, with 2,100 men, was despatched by Santa Anna to Texas to enforce these despotic laws.

Gen. Coss was met at San Antonio de Bexar, by Gen. Burleson, with about 600 men; Coss had garrisoned himself in the Alamo, and a bombardment was commenced and kept up by Gen. Burleson for several days, when his ammunition being nearly exhausted and his troops worn out, he ordered a retreat.

Col. Benj. Milam, who had recently escaped Mexican captivity, (having the marks of his galling chains yet upon him,) was not willing to raise the siege, and called upon the men under his command to stand by him, and he would yet defeat the enemy. About 160 or 170 obeyed his call, and he, with this handful of brave followers, continued the siege, and after a bombardment of four days, Gen. Coss and all his army surrendered at discression. The brave and heroic Col. Milam fell during this siege, as well as three of his brave followers. The loss on the Mexican side was very great.

Gen. Coss and his army declared for the republican constitution, and pledged themselves to its support, they were discharged on parol. This was in October 1835.

At this time, the Texas Provisional Congress was in session, and as before mentioned passed laws for the temporary government of Texas, and declared for the Republican Constitution of Mexico, which Santa Anna had succeeded in overthrowing. In

81

this Texas confidently expected to be joined by the republican party that had just been defeated in Mexico; but they now being all disarmed and their leaders discouraged, they failed to do so.

On the return of Gen. Coss to Mexico, he met Santa Anna at the head of 10,000 troops, chosen men, on his way to wage a war of extermination against Texas. Coss, and his troops joined Santa Anna, and notwithstanding their pledge to the contrary, took up arms against Texans, and in favor of the dictator.

Early in the spring of 1835, Santa Anna reached San Antonio de Bexar, where was garrisoned, in the same Alamo, Coss had surrendered, Cols. Travis, Bowie and Crockett, with about 180 men. The Alamo, after a severe and bloody battle, was defeated, and every one of its brave defenders inhumanly butchered.

Mrs. Dickerson, the wife of Capt. Dickerson, who fell in the Alamo, was sent on by Santa Anna, in company with Col. Travis' servant, to herald the news of the defeat of the Alamo, which soon spread through the country; and the force under Santa Anna, which though large, being greatly over-rated, the inhabitants were thrown into consternation, and the whole country, as it were, fled before the enemy. Gen. Houston was now raising an army, which, by the 15th of April, numbered about 2,000 men, all volunteers.

About the 20th of March, a part of Santa Anna's army attacked Goliad, where Col. Fannin, with about 300 men was stationed, who, after a brave and desperate defence, were forced to retreat. The enemy pursued and overtook Fannin and his army a few miles from Goliad, where they were all slain or taken prisoners. The prisoners, among whom was Col. Fannin, although they were told they should be treated as prisoners of war, were afterwards inhumanly butchered.

This second defeat added new terror to the almost defenceless inhabitants, and to describe the scene that now ensued would occupy many pages. The men were flocking around their country's standard, whilst the women and children were deserting their homes and fleeing in despair to the interior settlements and cities. Some with a sled and a pair of oxen, others with a small wood-wagon, and a few with carts, into which they had thrown such of their household effects as they most needed. The rivers and creeks being full from the spring flood, the progress of the fleeing women and children was both tedious and dangerous. In many places, they were compelled to travel in water two or three feet deep for several miles. Many of them lost their horses and oxen by their being bogged; whilst others were compelled to throw away their little effects, in order to lighten their loads so as to be able to progress at all.

It is impossible to describe, fully, the heart-rending scene that was here presented. Santa Anna's army burnt the houses of the citizens, killed their stock, and destroyed every thing before them, leaving behind nothing but desolation.

Gen. Houston was at Gonzales when the Alamo was defeated, and as the Mexican army advanced, he found it expedient to retreat, until he had passed the Colorado river, and from thence to the Brazos river. During this retreat his men were deserting by hundreds,* so that his army was reduced to less than 1000 men.

Whilst on the Brazos, Gen. Houston heard that Santa Anna had crossed the Brazos below, and was on his way to Galveston. He now ordered a forced march, and on the 19th of April, reached within a few miles of the Mexican army, which was encamped in the forks of San Jacinto river and Buffalo Bayou. Gen. Houston encamped within sight of the Mexican army, and for two days there was some firing between them, but no serious fighting. On the morning of the 21st, Gen. Rusk went to Gen. Houston and told him that unless the battle was fought that day, they would not have 100 men left; the army being now reduced to six hundred and fifty or seven hundred, and the men hourly deserting.

About two o'clock that day, Gen. Houston, having made every arrangement, headed his little band of brave hearted men, and, "ALAMO and FANNIN," being the watch-ward, they charged upon the enemy like hungry lions, and pouring a deadly fire into their ranks, strewed the ground with the slain. The first fire was returned, but without effect. On went the brave Texans until they reached the enemy's breast-works, which they mounted, and their deafening huzzas for victory were soon drowned by the simultaneous roar of their second fire. The Mexican army was completely over-awed, and as the Texans rushed upon them, pistol and knife in hand, they gave way. A promiscuous slaughter now ensued. Santa Anna, it is believed,

---

*It is, perhaps, proper and necessary that I should, in justice to many of the unfortunate deserters, remark that many of them had wives and children; and as the army was retreating, they found their homes deserted; their wives and little children having fled, whither they knew not; and it was to seek and relieve them that they deserted, and not from cowardice or any want of patriotism.

83

fell among the slain, and pretended to be dead, until the Texan army passed over them in pursuit of the retreating Mexicans, and then took to the prairies.

On account of the sudden and desperate attack made upon the Mexicans they did not run far, but fell upon their knees and begged for quarters. So exasperated were the Texans, that they could not be governed, but rushed upon them, and many were cut down before the officers could interfere, and stop the slaughter. There were about 800 of the enemy left dead on the ground, and about 800 taken prisoners, whilst Gen. Houston had only two men killed and four or five wounded. Upon this battle hung the destinies of Texas, and by it was gained her independence.

There appears to be an impression in the minds of many, that the conduct of Gen. Houston, previous to, and during this battle, was both reprehensible and cowardly. Much has also been said on this subject, through the public press, which was calculated to confirm this impression.

At the time of the battle, I was at Parker's Fort, and of course can say nothing as to his conduct, of my own knowledge; but from a personal and intimate acquaintance with Gen. Houston of 15 years, I can confidently assert, what, I believe not a single man who knows him, or who was in this battle will deny, that he is *not a coward!* and, with the exception of a few of his enemies, all agree that God never made a braver man.

It is true that Gen. Houston's conduct in retreating before the enemy had the appearance of indiscretion; but he knew what he was about, and it is now confidently believed that·had he gone into this battle sooner than he did, he would have been defeated. His conviction of this fact, and the great responsibility he felt, induced him to act as he did, and by thus acting, he gained the independence of Texas, saved his brave men from slaughter, and preseved the inhabitants from a war of extermination, which Santa Anna had declared it should be.

There are other insignificant charges against the character of this great and good man, which it is not my purpose to notice —neither is it necessary, for Gen. Houston, like the illustrious Washington, may truly be said to be "first in war—first in peace, and first in the hearts of his countrymen." Gen. Washington had his enemies—so has Gen. Houston. Gen. Washington's name is treasured in the hearts of his countrymen, whilst the names of his traducers are forgotten, or are only remembered as by-words. The same will be the case with Gen. Houston. Long after the names of his enemies have sunk into oblivion, his will be fresh in the minds of the patriots and freemen of every clime, and cherished with feelings of gratitude in all time by those who will reap the benefit of his valor.

Gen. Houston's moral character, may, in past times, have been censurable, but with this exception, (and all men have had, at some period of their lives, objectionable traits in their character) he has occupied a position far beyond the poisonous arrows of malice, and the unholy vituperations of envy. For morality and sobriety, he now stands as high as any man in any country. As a husband, one of the most accomplished and estimable ladies in the world, bears evidence of his affection and care—as a neighbor, there are none who have had the opportunity, but have been the recipients of his kindnesses and good offices, and as a friend, none are more sincere and valued. But to return from this digression.

Santa Anna, as before mentioned, finding that the brave Texans had overpowed his vandal followers, hastily prepared himself with a soldiers dress and fled through the prairie. He remained out on leg bail until the following day, when Mr. Silvester, from the State of Ohio, with a few other men, found his dictatorship snugly ensconsed in a marsh. When he was taken, his captors charged him with being Gen. Santa Anna, but he protested he was not. He had unfortunately, however, in exchanging his clothing, neglected to change his shirt, and he was asked if the Mexican soldiers wore as fine shirts as the one he had on? He now confessed, with tears in his eyes, that he was one of Santa Anna's Aids, and begged to be taken to Gen. Houston. To this timely foresight, in becoming an aid instead of being a general, he owes his life.

How changed—what a ridiculous aspect did this great General and Dictator of Mexico, present. But a few days since, and arrayed in all his grandeur, he urged his servile troops on to the most inhuman butchery of the brave Crockett, Travis, Bowie and others, at the Alamo—but yesterday, as it were, and he stood in security, amidst his Aids, and ordered, and looked with coolness upon the slaughter of Fannin and his men—and now he stands, covered with filth and dirt, a poor suppliant for his life, at the hands of an inferior officer of the Texas army.

When Santa Anna was brought before Gen. Houston, he received him and treated him in that manner his station, as a prisoner of war, demanded. After retaining him for a month or two, as a prisoner of war, he was permited to return to Mexico. How differently would he have treated Gen. Houston, had the god of war reversed their situations; he, no doubt, would have had him shot, in a few hours after the battle. The heart of a brave man never delights in cruelty to his vanquished foe, but the heart of a coward does.

Peace being once more restored in Texas, the citizens again returned to their homes. Many found their houses a heap of ashes, their horses, cattle and hogs, either driven off, or killed. It was truly distressing to witness the return of the unfortunate inhabitants to their now desolate homes. I say it was distressing, because of the contrast they now presented, to their appearence when they left them a few weeks past. Then they left comfortable houses, farms well stocked and fine crops growing, all giving promise of comfort, plenty and happiness—they now returned to take shelter under a temporary shed, whilst many of them had no bed but the cold ground, and their only shelter, the arched canopy of heaven—their pastures were herdless, and their crops destroyed.

It is easy for the reader to conjecture what was the pecuniary condition of Texas at this time. Like her mother republic, the United States, when she threw off the yoke of British bondage, she was poor indeed; but the eagle of liberty was now hovering over this "lone star republic," and cheered on her hardy sons and daughters in their darkest hours of despair, 'til, through the merciful beneficence of a kind Providence, they are once more surrounded by most of the comforts and blessings of this life.

Since the battle of San Jacinto, there has been no very serious disturbance between Mexico and Texas. Under the administration President Miraubo B. Lamar, an expedition was fitted out to go to Santa Fe, in order to extend the jurisdiction of Texas over it. This expedition was under the command of General McLeod. He had progressed as far as the northwestern table-lands, where, having divided his company, which numbered about three hundred men, he was defeated, and all his men either killed or taken prisoners. This, with the exception of the disturbances from a few marauding parties of Mexicans that now and then came into the western frontiers, but soon returned without commiting serious injury, are all the difficulties this country has experienced since the battle of San Jacinto.

There remain but two obstacles to the immediate rapid progress of Texas to wealth and greatness, and these will no doubt soon be removed, viz: the hostility of the Indians and opposition of Mexico to her independence. That permanent and honorable treaties will soon be formed with the former, and that the latter will ere long acknowledge her independence, there is no doubt.

There has been much said, and much continues to be said, both in the United States and Texas, on the subject of annexing the latter to the former. What may be the final result of the negotiations now pending between the two governments on that subject, can not be foreseen—nor is it of much importance to the Republic of Texas how it is decided. The day has been, when the citizens of Texas were anxious to be annexed to the United States; but it is now getting late in the afternoon of that day. They look upon the United States as their common parent. There are few of her citizens, who are not bound to the United States by the strongest ties of affection—it was here they were born, and here they now have many near and dear relatives and friends—it was here that they first breathed the uncontaminated atmosphere of freedom and independence, and it was here they imbibed that spirit which caused them to resist the encroachments of despotism upon their adopted soil, and nerved their arms upon the field of battle. It was in defense of those principles of republican liberty, which they sucked from their mothers' breasts, that led them to enrich, with their blood, and whiten with their bones, the plains of Goliad, San Antonio, and San Jacinto. But whilst the indomitable citizens of the Lone Star Republic will emulate the virtues, honor the high standing, and rejoice at the prosperity of their mother republic, they will *never*, NO, NEVER! pay a vile obeisance to any power upon earth, in order to secure their alliance or gain their favor. The fate of the treaty now under consideration, will decide the question of annexation once and forever, so far as Texas is concerned. The morn of her greatness has already dawned, and the sun of her glory will soon rise in all its beauty and grandeur.

The best land route to Texas from the western parts of Missouri, Arkansas and Wisconsin, is through Arkansas by way of Van Buren and Fort Smith to the Military Road. Thence, through the Choctaw nation* to Fort Towson.

From the eastern parts of these and all north, the emigrant should cross the Mississippi at St. Genevieve, taking the following places in his route: St. Michael, Batesville, on White river, and Little Rock, to Washington in Hemsted county, Arkansas.

Emigrants from the Eastern or Southern States, should cross Red river at either of the following points: Alexandria, Natchitoches, or Shreveport .

In going by sea to eastern Texas, ship at New Orleans for Sabine city; to Middle Texas, for Galveston; to Western Texas, for Matagorda, Linville, or Live Oak Point.

The time at sea, in going to Sabine city, is six hours; to Galveston, thirty-six hours; to Matagorda, sixty hours.

---

* The Chottaw Indians are perfectly friendly, and some of them are very wealthy. Some white men have married among these Indians who cultivate large farms. They boast that they have never shed the blood of a white man. The facilities for obtaining provisions of all kinds, are abundant here.

Narrative of the Capture and Subsequent Sufferings

OF

Mrs. Rachel Plummer

During a Captivity of Twenty-one Months Among
The Comanche Indians; With a Sketch of
Their Manners, Customs, Laws,
&c., &.

WITH

A Short Description of the Country Over Which
She Traveled Whilst With the Indians.

Written By Herself.

1839

Mrs. Rachel Lofton, Greatgranddaughter of James W. Parker, owner of the Trusty Rifle, spoken of in the little book, with the rifle in hand.

PREFACE

In my preface to the first edition of this narrative, I promised a second edition, should the first meet with public patronage. The patronage extended to it has far exceeded my most sanguine expectations, for which I embrace the present opportunity to return my most sincere thanks to my friends and the public in general. In redemption of my promise, I present this second edition, revised and corrected, confidently anticipating the favorable consideration and renewed patronage of a generous public.

I hope it is unnecessary to ask my readers to throw over my awkward phraseology, ungrammatical sentences, and uncouth style, the veil of charity, as they cannot but recognize, at once, my want of education and practical experience in writing. Should this humble narrative be read with a critic's eye, and feeling injustice will be done me, and the object I have in view, in again appearing before the public will fail of being attained, viz: 1st. To make the reader acquainted with the manners and customs of the largest nation of Indians upon the American continent. 2nd. To warn all who are, or may be placed in a situation where they may be liable to fall a prey to savage barbarity, of what I have suffered, and thus induce them to avoid my fate; whilst at the same time I hope to excite a sympathy for those who are now, or hereafter may be prisoners among the Indians, and thus induce greater efforts for their release. 3rd. To briefly describe a country, yet known to but few of my readers, and which is destined, at no distant day, to excite much interest among the inhabitants of the United States and Texas.

With these remarks, I submit the following pages to the perusal of a generous public, feeling assured that before they are published, the hand that penned them will be cold in death.

RACHEL PLUMMER.

City of Houston, Texas, Dec. 3, 1839.

91

NARRATIVE

On the 19th of May, 1836, I was living in Fort Parker, on the head waters of the river Navasott. My father, (James W. Parker,) and my husband and brother-in-law were cultivating my father's farm, which was about a mile from the fort. In the morning, say 9 o'clock, my father, husband, brother-in-law, and brother, went to the farm to work. I do not think they had left the fort more than an hour before some one of the fort cried out, "Indians!" The inmates of the fort had retired to their farms in the neighborhood, and there were only six men in it, viz: my grandfather, Elder John Parker, my two uncles, Benjamin and Silas Parker, Samuel Frost and his son Robert, and Frost's son-in-law, G. E. Dwight. All appeared in a state of confusion, for the Indians (numbering something not far from eight hundred) had raised a white flag.

On the first sight of the Indians, my sister (Mrs. Nixon,) started to alarm my father and his company at the farm, whilst the Indians were yet more than a quarter of a mile from the fort, and I saw her no more. I was in the act of starting to the farm, but I knew I was not able to take my little son, (James Pratt Plummer.) The women were all soon gone from the fort, whither I did not know; but I expected towards the farm. My old grandfather and grandmother, and several others, started through the farm, which was immediately adjoining the fort. Dwight started with his family and Mrs. Frost and her little children. As he started, uncle Silas said, "Good Lord, Dwight, you are not going to run? He said, "No, I am only going to try to hide the women and children in the woods." Uncle said, "Stand and fight like a man, and if we have to die we will sell our lives as dearly as we can.

The Indians halted; and two Indians came up to the fort to inform the inmates that they were friendly, and had come for the purpose of making a treaty with the Americans. This instantly threw the people off their guard, and uncle Benjamin went to the Indians, who had now got within a few hundred yards of the fort. In a few minutes he returned, and told Frost and his son and uncle Silas that he believed the Indians intended to fight, and told them to put every thing in the best order for defence. He said he would go back to the Indians and see if the fight could be avoided. Uncle Silas told him not to go, but to try to defend the place as well as they could; but he started off again to the Indians, and appeared to pay but little attention to what Silas said. Uncle Silas said, "I know they will kill Benjamin;" and said to me, "do you stand here and watch the Indians' motions until I run into my house"—I think he said for his shot pouch. I suppose he had got a wrong shot-pouch as he had four or five rifles. When uncle Benjamin reached the body of Indians they turned to the right and left and surrounded him. I was now satisfied they intended killing him. I took up my little James Pratt, and thought I would try to make my escape. As I ran across the fort, I met Silas returning to the place where he left me. He asked me if they had killed Benjamin. I told him, "No; but they have surrounded him." He said, "I know they will kill him, but I will be good for one of them at least." These were the last words I heard him utter.

I ran out of the fort, and passing the corner I saw the Indians drive their spears into Benjamin. The work of death had already commenced. I shall not attempt to describe their terrific yells, their united voices that seemed to reach the very skies, whilst they were dealing death to the inmates of the fort. It can scarcely be comprehended in the wide field of imagination. I know it is utterly impossible for me to give every particular in detail, for I was much alarmed.

I tried to make my escape, but alas, alas, it was too late, as a party of the Indians had got ahead of me. Oh! how vain were my feeble efforts to try to run to save myself and little James Pratt. A large sulky looking Indian picked up a hoe and knocked me down. I well recollect of their taking my child out of my arms, but whether they hit me any more I do not know, for I swooned away. The first I recollect, they were dragging me along by the hair. I made several unsuccessful attempts to raise to my feet before I could do it. As they took me past the fort, I heard an awful screaming near the place where they had first seized me.* I heard some shots. I then heard uncle Silas shout a triumphant huzza! I did, for one moment, hope the men had gathered from the neighboring farms, and might release me.

I was soon dragged to the main body of the Indians, where they had killed uncle Benjamin. His face was much mutilated, and many arrows were sticking in his body. As the savages

* I think Uncle Silas was trying to release me, and in doing this he lost his life; but not until he had killed four Indians.

passed by, they thrust their spears through him. I was covered with blood, for my wound was bleeding freely. I looked for my child but could not see him, and was convinced they had killed him, and every moment expected to share the same fate myself. At length I saw him. An Indian had him on his horse; he was calling, mother, oh, mother! He was just able to lisp the name of mother, being only about 18 months old. There were two Comanche women with them, (their battles are always brought on by a woman,) one of whom came to me and struck me several times with a whip. I suppose it was to make me quit crying.

I now expected my father and husband, and all the rest of the men were killed. I soon saw a party of the Indians bringing my aunt Elizabeth Kellogg and uncle Silas' two oldest children, Cynthia Ann, and John; also some bloody scalps; among them I could distinguish that of my grandfather by the grey hairs, but could not discriminate the balance.

Most of the Indians were engaged in plundering the fort. They cut open our bed ticks and threw the feathers in the air, which was literally thick with them. They brought out a great number of my father's books and medicines. Some of the books were torn up, and most of the bottles of medicine were broken; though they took on some for several days*

I had few minutes to reflect, for they soon started back the same way they came up. As I was leaving, I looked back at the place where I was one hour before, happy and free, and now in the hands of a ruthless, savage enemy.

They killed a great many of our cattle as they went along. They soon convinced me that I had no time to reflect upon the past, for they commenced whipping and beating me with clubs, &c., so that my flesh was never well from bruises and wounds during my captivity. To undertake to narrate their barbarous treatment would only add to my present distress, for it is with feelings of the deepest mortification that I think of it, much less to speak or write of it; for while I record this painful part of my narrative; I can almost fell the same heart-rending pains of body and mind that I then endured, my very soul becomes sick at the dreadful thought.

---

* Among them was a bottle of pulverized arsenic, which the Indians mistook for a kind of white paint, with which they painted their faces and bodies all over, after dissolving it in their saliva. The bottle was brought to me to tell them what it was. I did not do it, though I knew it, for the bottle was labeled. Four of the Indians painted themselves with it as above described, and it did not fail to kill them.

About midnight they stopped. They now tied a plaited thong around my arms, and drew my hands behind me. They tied them so tight that the scars can be easily seen to this day. They then tied a similar thong around my ankles, and drew my feet and hands together. They now turned me on my face and I was unable to trun over, when they commenced beating me over the head with their bows, and it was with great difficuty I could keep from smothering in my blood; for the wound they gave me with the hoe, and many others, were bleeding freely.

I suppose it was to add to my misery that they brought my little James Pratt so near me that I could hear him cry. He would call for mother; and often was his voice weakened by the blows they would give him. I could hear the blows. I could hear his cries; but oh, alas, could offer him no relief. The rest of the prisoners were brought near me, but we were not allowed to speak one word together. My aunt called me once, and I answered her; but, indeed, I thought she would never call or I answer again, for they jumped with their feet upon us, which nearly took our lives. Often did the children cry, but were soon hushed by such blows that I had no idea they could survive. They commenced screaming and dancing around the scalps; kicking and stamping the prisoners.

I now ask you, my christian reader, to pause. You who are living secure from danger—you who have read the sacred scriptures of truth—who have been raised in a land boasting of christian philanthropy—I say, I now ask you to form some idea of what my feelings were. Such dreadful savage yelling! enough to terrify the bravest hearts. Bleeding and weltering in my blood; and far worse, to think of my little darling Pratt! Will this scene ever be effaced from my memory? Not until my spirit is called to leave this tenement of clay; and may God grant me a heart to pray for them, for "they know not what they do."

Next morning, they started in a northern direction. They tied me every night, as before stated, for five nights. During the first five days, I never ate one mouthful of food, and had but a very scanty allowance of water. Notwithstanding my sufferings, I could not but admire the country—being prairie and timber, and very rich. I saw many fine springs. It was some 70 or 80 miles from the fort to the Cross Timbers. This is a range of timber-land from the waters of Arkansas, bearing a southwest direction, crossing the False Ouachita, Red River, the heads

95

of Sabine, Angelina, Natchitoches, Trinity, Brazos, Colorado, &c., going on southwest, quite to the Rio Grande. The range of timber is of an irregular width, say from 5 to 35 miles wide, and is a very diversified country; abounding with small prairies, skirted with timber of various kinds—oak, of every description, ash, elm, hickory, walnut and mulberry. There is more post oak on the uplands than any other kind; and a great deal of this range of timber land is very rough, bushy, abounds with briers, and some of it poor. West, or S. W. of the Brazos, it is very mountainous. As this range of timber reaches the waters of the Rio Grande, (Big River,) it appears to widen out, and is directly adjoining the timber covering the table lands between Austin and Santa Fe. This country, particularly southwest of the Brazos, is a well watered country, and part of it will be densely inhabited. The purest atmosphere I ever breathed was that of these regions.

After we reached the Grand Prairie, we turned more to the east; that is, the party I belonged to. Aunt Elizabeth fell to the Kitchawas, and my nephew and neice to another portion of the Comanches.

I must again call my reader to bear with me in rehearsing the continued barbarous treatment of the Indians. My child kept crying, and almost continually calling for "Mother," though I was not allowed even to speak to it. At the time they took off my fetters, they brought my child to me, supposing that I gave suck. As soon as it saw me, it, trembling with weakness, hastened to my embraces. Oh, with what feelings of love and sorrow did I embrace the mutilated body of my darling little James Pratt. I now felt that my case was much bettered, as I thought they would let me have my child; but oh, mistaken, indeed, was I; for as soon as they found that I had weaned him, they, in spite of all my efforts, tore him from my embrace. He reached out his hands towards me, which were covered with blood, and cried, "Mother, Mother, oh, Mother!" I looked after him as he was borne from me, and I sobbed aloud. This was the last I ever heard of my little Pratt. Where he is, I know not.

Progressing farther and farther from my home, we crossed Big Red River, the head of Arkansas, and then turned more to the northwest. We now lost sight of timber entirely.

For several hundred miles after we had left the Cross Timber country, and on the Red River, Arkansas, &c., there is a fine country. The timber is scarce and scrubby. Some streams as salt as brine; and others, fine water. The land, in part, is very rich, and game plenty.

We would travel for weeks and not see a riding switch. Buffalo dung is all the fuel. This is gatherd into a round pile; and when set on fire, it does very well to cook by, and will keep fire for several days.

In July, and in part of August, we were on the Snow Mountains. There it is perpetual snow; and I suffered more from cold than I ever suffered in my life before. It was very seldom I had any thing to put on my feet, but very little covering for my body. I had to mind the horses every night, and had a certain number of buffalo skins to dress every moon. This kept me employed all the time in day-light; and often would I have to take my buffalo skin with me, to finish it whilst I was minding the horses. My feet would be often frozen, even while I would be dressing skins, and I dared not complain; for my situation still grew more and more difficult.

In October, I gave birth to my second son. As to the months, &c., it was guess work with me, for I had no means of keeping the time. It was an interesting and beautiful babe. I had, as you may suppose, but a very poor chance to comfort myself with any thing suitable to my situation, or that of my little infant. The Indians were not as hostile now as I had feared they would be. I was still fearful they would kill my child; and having now been with them some six months, I had learned their language. I would often expostulate with my mistress* to advise me what to do to save my child; but all in vain. My child was some six or seven weeks old, when I suppose my master thought it too much trouble, as I was not able to go through as much labor as before. One cold morning, five or six large Indians came where I was suckling my infant. As soon as they came in I felt my heart sick; my fears agitated my whole frame to a complete state of convulsion; my body shook with fear indeed. Nor were my fears vain or ill-grounded. One of them caught hold of the child by the throat; and with his whole strength, and like an enraged lion actuated by its devouring nature, held on like the hungry vulture, until my child was to all appearance entirely dead. I exerted my whole feeble strength

---

* Having fallen into the hands of an old man that had only his wife and one daughter, who composed his family, I was compelled to reverence the both women as mistresses.

to relieve it; but the other Indians held me. They, by force, took it from me, and threw it up in the air, and let it fall on the frozen ground, until it was apparently dead.

They gave it back to me. The fountain of tears that had hitherto given vent to my grief, was now dried up. While I gazed upon the bruised cheeks of my darling infant, I discovered some symptoms of returning life. Oh, how vain was my hope that they would let me have it if I could revive it. I washed the blood from its face; and after some time, it began to breathe again; but a more heart-rending scene ensued. As soon as they found it had recovered a little, they again tore it from my embrace and knocked me down. They tied a platted rope round the child's neck, and drew its naked body into the large hedges of prickly pears, which were from eight to twelve feet high. They would then pull it down through the pears. This they repeated several times. One of them then got on a horse, and tying the rope to his saddle, rode round a circuit of a few hundred yards, until my little innocent one was not only dead, but literally torn to pieces. I stood horror struck. One of them then took it up by the leg, brought it to me, and threw it into my lap. But in praise to the Indians, I must say, that they gave me time to dig a hole in the earth and bury it. After having performed this last service to the lifeless remains of my dear babe, I sat down and gazed with joy on the resting place of my now happy infant; and I could, with old David, say, "You cannot come to me, but I must go to you;" and then, and even now, whilst I record the awful tragedy, I rejoice that it has passed from the sufferings and sorrows of this world. I shall hear its deathly cries no more; and fully and confidently believing, and solely relying on the imputed righteousness of God in Christ Jesus, I feel that my happy babe is now with its kindred spirits in that eternal world of joys. Oh! will my dear Saviour, by his grace, keep me through life's short journey, and bring me to dwell with my happy children in the sweet realms of endless bliss, where I shall meet the whole family of Heaven—those whose names are recorded in the Lamb's Book of Life.

I would have been glad to have had the pleasure of laying my little James Pratt with this my happy infant. I do really believe I could have buried him without shedding a tear; for, indeed, they had ceased to flow in relief of my grief. My heaving bosom could do no more than breathe deep sighs. Parents, you little know what you can bear. Surely, surely, my poor heart must break.

We left this place and as usual, were again on a prairie, We soon discovered a large lake of water. I was very thirsty; and although we traveled directly towards it, we could never get any nearer to it. It did not appear to be more than forty or fifty steps off, and always kept the same distance. This astonished me beyond measure. Is there any thing like magic in this, said I. I never saw a lake, pond, or river, plainer in my life. My thirst was excessive, and I was panting for a drop of water; but I could get no nearer to it. I found it to be a kind of gas, as I supposed, and I leave the reader to put his own construction upon it. It is, by some, called water gas. It looks just like water, and appears even to show the waves. I have often seen large herds of Buffalo feeding in it. They appeared as if they were wading in the water; and their wakes looked as distinct as in real water.*

In those places, the prairies are as level as the surface of a lake, and can better be described by at once imagining yourself looking at a large lake. I have but a faint idea of the cause; but from the number of sea shells, (oyters', &c.,) I have no doubt that this great prairie was once a sea.

I was often on the salt plains. There the salt some little resembles dirty snow on a very cold day, being very light. The wind will blow it for miles. I have seen it in many places half leg deep; whilst other parts of the ground would be naked, owing to the strong winds drifting it.

I was at some of the salt lakes, which are very interesting to the view. Thousands of bushels of salt—yea, millions—resembling ice; a little on the muddy or milky order. It appears that there would not be consumption for this immense amount of salt in all the world; for it forms anew when it is removed, so that it is inexhaustible.

These prairies abound with such a number and variety of beasts, that pages could not describe them.

1st. The little prairie dog is as large as a gray squirrel. Some of them are as spotted as a leopard; but they are mostly of a dark color, and live in herds. They burrow in the ground. As a stranger approaches them, they set up a loud barking; but

---

* This was the mirage, common to large deserts and prairies. Those travelers in the East, who have passed over the deserts of Asia and Africa, make frequent mention of these phenomena.

will soon sink down into their holes. They are very fat, and fine to eat.

2nd. The prairie fox is a curious animal. It is as tall as a small dog—its body not larger than a grey squirrel, but three times as long. Their legs are remarkably small; being but little larger than a large straw. They can run very fast. Seldom fat.

3rd. The rabbit rivals the snow in whiteness, and is as large as a small dog. They are very active, and are delicious to eat. They can run very fast. I have thought they were the most beautiful animal I ever saw.

4th. The mountain sheep are smaller than the common sheep, and have long hair. They will feed on the brink of the steepest precipice, and are very active. They are very plentiful about the mountians.

5th. Buffalo, the next largest animal known, except the elephant. Their number no one can tell. They are found in the prairies and seldom in the timber even when there is any. Their flesh is the most delicious of all the beef kind I have seen. I have often seen the ground covered with them as far as the eye could reach.

The Indians shoot them with their arrows from their horses. They kill them very fast, and will even shoot an arrow entirely through one of these large animals.

6th. The Elk, the largest of the deer species, with very large horns, and often more than six feet long. There are but few of them found in the same country with the buffalo; but they range along the Missouri river in parts of the Rocky Mountains. Their flesh is like venison.

7th. The Antelope. This is, I believe, the fleetest animal in the world. They go in large flocks or herds. They will see the stranger a great way off, will run towards him till they get within twenty or thirty steps, and then the whole herd (perhaps some thousands) will wheel at the same moment, and are soon two or three miles off. They will again approach you, but not quite so near as at first, and then wheel again. They generally make about three or four of these visits, still wheeling from you at a greater distance. They will then leave you. They are much like the goat, and are by some called the wild goat.

8th. There are a great variety of wolves on the prairies; the large grey wolf, the large black wolf, the prairie wolf, and,

I believe, the proper jackall. There is a large white wolf which will weigh 300 pounds, has very long hair of silvery white, and is very ferocious. They will kill a buffalo, and will not go out of the way of man or beast.

9th. There are four kinds of bears in the mountains; the white, grisley, red, and black bears. The grisley bear is the largest and most powerful. They will weigh 1200 or 1400 pounds. They cannot climb, but live in the valleys about the mountains. They are very delicious food. The white bear is very ferocious, and will attack either man or beast. They are hard to conquer. The Indians are very fearful of them, and will not attack them; and even if attacked by them, will try to make their escape. They are of a silvery white, and are found along the brows of the Rocky Mountains. They are very fat and delicious food. The common black bear is scarce, as is also the red bear. The last species of bear is alone heard of in the western part of the Rocky Mountains. They are the most beautiful beast I ever saw, being red as vermillion.

10th. The common deer is in many places very plenty. In the mountains they grow much larger than they do in Texas.

11th. Turkeys, on the heads of Columbia river, are very numerous. They do not range on the prairies nor about the Snow mountains.

12th. Wild horses (Mustangs) are very plenty on the prairies. Thousands of the very finest horses, mules, jacks, &c., may be seen in one day. They are very wild. The Indians often take them by running them on their horses and throwing the lasso over their heads. They are easily domesticated.

13th. Man-Tiger. The Indians say that they have found several of them in the mountains. They describe them as being of the feature and make of a man. They are said to walk erect, and are eight or nine feet high. Instead of hands, they have huge paws and long claws, with which they can easily tear a buffalo to pieces. The Indians are very shy of them, and whilst in the mountains, will never separate. They also assert that there is a species of human beings that live in the caves in the mountains. They describe them to be not more than three feet high. They say that these little people are alone found in the country where the man-tiger frequents, and that the former takes cognizance of them, and will destroy any thing that attempts to harm them.

101

14th. The beaver is found in great numbers in the ponds, which are very numerous on the heads of the Columbia, Missouri, Arkansas, Rio Grande, Platte, and all the country between; though it is very mountainous, and sometimes the ponds are on the highest ground.

These strange animals, in many instances, appear to possess the wisdom of human beings. They appear to have their family connections, and each family lives separate, sometimes numbering more than a hundred in a family. A stranger is not allowed to dwell with them. They burrow in the ground when they cannot get timber to build huts. In case they can get timber, they will cut down quite large trees with their teeth, then cut them off in lengths to suit their purposes; sometimes five or six feet long, and will then unite in hauling them to a chosen spot, and build up their houses in the edge of the water. The first story of some three feet high—one door under the water. The next story is not so high, has three doors, one next the water, one next the land, and one down through the floor into the first story. There is continually a sentinel at the door next the land, and on the approach of any thing that alarms them, they are soon in the water.

They will move from one pond to another, and it is strange to see what a large road they make in removing. Their fur and size need no description. They are generally very fat, but the tail only is fit to eat. The bait with which the traps are baited, is collected from this animal, and is difficult to prepare, as there has to be a precise amount of certain parts of the animal. If there is too much of any one ingredient they will become alarmed, and even leave the pond. In preparing the bait, no part of your flesh must touch it, or they will not come near it. The bait has to be changed every few days by adding something; a small piece of spignard or annis root may be dropped into it. It is kept close in bladders, or skin bags, and nothing that goes into it must be touched with the hands.

15th. Muskrats in those ponds are beyond number. They also build houses in the ponds. They are built of any kind of trash they can find.

The most abrupt range of the Rocky Mountains embraces a large tract of country, and so incredibly high, and perpendicular are they in many places, that it is impossible to ascend them. At some places the tall sharp peaks of mountains resemble much the steeple on a church. Probably you can see twenty of these

102

high peaks at one sight; and in other places the steep rock bluff, perhaps 200 feet high, will extend ten miles perfectly strait and uniform. In some places you will find a small tract of level country on the tops of the mountains. These levels are generally very rich. This range of mountains crosses the heads of the Missouri, and bears in a southwesterly direction to, and beyond the Rio Grande, even as far as I have ever been; also, bearing north, down the Columbia river as far as I went, and the head waters of the Platte, (perhaps I may be mistaken in the names of some of the rivers.) They can better be described by saying they are a dreadful rough range of mountains, I suppose as high as any others in the world. The bottoms are very rich. It will be winter on the top of the mountains, and spring or summer in the valleys. There is a kind of wild flax that grows in these bottoms which yields a lint, out of which the Indians make ropes. It is very strong. As far as I was down on the tributaries of the Columbia, the bottoms were seldom more than one half mile wide; in some places a mile. The timber is indifferent in the bottoms, and more indifferent on the high land.

The buffalo sometimes finds it very difficult to ascend or descend these mountains, I have sometimes amused myself by getting on the top of one of these high pinnacles and looking over the country. You can see one mountain beyond another until they are lost in the misty air. Where you can see the valleys, you will often see them literally covered with the buffalo, sometimes the elk, wild horse, &c.

Northwest of the head of the Rio Grande, which is some 150 miles N. W. of Santa Fe, the country becomes more level. Part of this country is inhabited by a nation of Indians, called Apatches, and another tribe called Ferbelows. In this section of country there are some farms where fine wheat is raised.

This region of country is but very little known by the American people, being infested with such numerous tribes of Indians that Americans are very unsafe to be there. If the timber was not so indifferent, this country would be densely inhabited. The soil would fully justify the idea. In point of health it certainly is not surpassed in the world; and although very far to the north, is not excessively cold. I do not think it is colder than the state of Tennessee. The present inhabitants say there is nothing like fevers known in that country.

103

There are a great many caves in this high mountainous country. I must give my readers an account of one of my adventures in one of these caves. I am compelled to ask my reader to indulge me in the following adventure, as I am certain that this, as well as others of my adventures, will appear very remarkable; and reader, you will be compelled to fancy yourself in a condition where life has lost its sweetness, before you will be able to credit it. And here let me remark, that I have withheld stating many things, that are facts, because I well know that you will doubt whether any person could survive what I have undergone. I further assure you, my reader, that I have not written one word but what is fact. But to my story.

At one time, whilst on the Rocky Mountains, I had discovered a cave near the foot of the mountain. Having noticed some singular rocks, &c., at its mouth, that excited in me curiosity to explore this singular looking place, and the time drawing nigh, that we were to leave this encampment, I was much afraid I would not have an an opportunity of satisfying this curiosity. I had repeatedly asked my mistress to permit me to go into the cave, but she refused. A few days before we were to leave, however, she yielded a reluctant consent to my singular desire, and also permitted my young mistress to accompany me.

I immediately set about making my arrangements for this adventure. I procured some buffalo tallow, and made of a part of it some large candles, (if I may so call them) and took with me some tallow to make more, should I need them. I took with me the necessary instruments for striking fire, procured some light fuel, and thus prepared, we started into the cave. We had not proceeded more than 30 or 40 rods, when my companion became alarmed. I told her there was nothing alarming yet, and tried to persuade her to go on with me, but she refused to go any farther herself, or to let me go. I was, however, determined to proceed, and she appeared determined that I should return. A combat now ensued, and she struck at me with a piece of the wood we had with us. I dodged the blow, and knocked her down with another piece. This made her yell most hideously; but being both out of sight and out of hearing of any person, I cared not for her cries, but firmly told her that if she attempted again to force me to return until I was ready, I would kill her. In the scuffle, being both down, the candle had fallen from my hand, and fortunately was not put out. I picked it up, and here a sight was presented to my view that surpasses all description. Innumerable stars, from the most diminutive size up to that of the full moon, studded the impenetrable gloom above and around us. I had not, until now, noticed the sublime and awful appearance of the cave. It was this sight that had alarmed my companion, and finding it impossible to induce her to proceed on the adventure with me, I agreed, on the condition that she would help me to mind the horses, to return with her to the mouth of the cave, which I did, and then returned to prosecute my adventure in the cave.

On reaching the battle-ground, I felt a great anxiety to find out the cause of this strange scene, which upon a close examination ,was more splendid than the mind can conceive. Reader, you may fancy yourself viewing, at once, an entirely new planetary system, a thousand times more sublime and more beautiful than our own, and you fall far short of the reality I here witnessed. I soon discovered that these lights proceeded from the reflections of the light of the candle by the almost innumerable chrystalized formations in the rocks above, and on either side. The room I was in was large, say 100 feet wide, and its length was beyond my sight. The ceiling was about twelve feet high, and the floor was nearly smooth, and in many places was as transparent as the clearest glass. The sides and ceiling were thickly set with the same material, from which projected thousands of knobs or lumps, varying from 1 to 30 inches in length. The reflections of the light of the candle, from these transparent lumps, exactly resembling the clearest ice, proved to be the stars that had caused so much alarm in my young mistress, and wonder in me. Having satisfied my curiosity by a full examination of this singular apartment, I pursued my journey in the bowels of the earth.

For a distance of three or four miles, the cave differed in appearance and width, but nothing worthy of notice was observed. I now came to another place that excited my admiration. The cave forked, the ceiling or roof of the right hand fork being about 10 feet high and 6 feet wide. This avenue was obstructed by the intervention of bars of these transparent formations, reaching from the ceiling to the floor. They were to close together to permit my body to pass beween them, and the room, into which I could look, surpassing, in splendor, any thing I had yet seen, I was anxious to explore it. After much labor, I succeeded in breaking one of these bars, and now entered one of the most spacious and splendid rooms my eyes ever beheld.

105

It was about 100 feet in diameter, and 10 feet high. It was nearly circular, and the walls, ceiling and floor being entirely transparent, presented a scene of which the mind can form no just conception, much less the pen describe. I know my readers would not credit if I were to attempt to describe it. I therefore leave my readers to their own conjectures of how a room would look, prepared as a house of public worship, with a pulpit and three rows of seats around it, all of the same material, as has been described, on one side, and on the other a beautiful clear stream of water.

The water of this river, or creek, was so clear that I could have seen a pin on the bottom. It was about 50 yards wide, and varied from one to two feet deep. I crossed it, and after going down it a mile or more, I heard most terrific roaring. I continued my course in the direction from whence it came until I reached a place where this stream fell down a precipice, the depth of which I could form no conjecture, but from deafening roar that it made, it must have been immense.

Being much fatigued, and having come to the end of my journey, I sat down to rest. I had not been seated here long before I fell asleep, as I suppose, and in the confused roar of the waters I fancied I could hear the dying screams of my infant. I thought of home and my friends far away, that I must never see again. My wounded body appeared to bleed afresh, as my mind reverted back to the cruelties inflicted upon me by my barbarian captivators, when there appeared to me the form of a human being. He held in his hand a bottle containing a liquid, with which he bathed my wounds, which ceased paining, and strange to say never hurt me afterwards. (This I know is not fancy, and sometimes, in reflecting upon this adventure, I am lost in doubt as to whether this whole scene was reality or only a dream.) He consoled me with kind words, that I well remember, but shall not here relate. Oh, could it have been possible that He who comforts the afflicted and gives strength to the weak, that God, in His bountiful mercy could have extended His hand to a poor wretch like me, whilst thus buried in the earth. How inscrutable are thy ways, Oh, God; and thy mercy and wisdom, how unsearchable. Were I to go give vent to my feelings, and possessed the mental capacity equal to the task, it would swell this humble narrative far beyond the limits I have prescribed to it.

106

Having renewed my light, I retraced my steps. I found the distance much greater, on returning, (or it appeared so,) than I thought. On reaching the place where my young mistress turned back, I found that the Indians had been in the cave looking for me. I reached the camp just as the sun was setting, and was astonished to learn that I had spent two days and one night in the cave. I never, in my life, had a more interesting adventure, and although I am now in the city of Houston, surrounded by friends and all the comforts of life, to sit alone, and in memory, retrace my steps in this cave, gives me more pleasurable feelings than all the gaudy show and pleasing gaiety with which I am surrounded. The impressions made upon my mind in this cave, have since served as a healing balm to my wounded soul.

There are some interesting incidents connected with this adventure, which I do not think proper to give the public at this time; they may, perhaps, be published hereafter. I have given but a very partial description of one of the most interesting scenes that occurred.

About the middle of March, all the Indian bands—that is, the Comanches, and all the hostile tribes, assembled and held a general war council. They met on the head waters of the Arkansas, and it was the largest assemblage I ever saw. The council was held upon a high eminence, descending every way. The encampments were as close as they could stand, and how far they extended I know not; for I could not see the outer edge of them with my naked eye.

I had now been with them so long that I had learned their language, and as the council was held in the Comanche language, I determined, (for I yet entertained a faint hope that I would be released,) to know the result of their proceedings. It being contrary to their laws to permit their squaws to be present in their councils, I was several times repulsed with blows, but I cheerfully submitted to abuse and persevered in listening to their proceedings.

A number of traditionary ceremonies were performed, such as would be of but little interest to the reader. This ceremony occupied about three days, after which they came to a determination to invade and take possession of Texas. It was agreed that those tribes of Indians who were in the habit of raising corn, should cultivate the farms of the people of Texas; the prairie Indians were to have entire control of the prairies, each

107

party to defend each other. After having taken Texas, killed and driven out the inhabitants, and the corn growing Indians had raised a good supply, they were to attack Mexico. There they expected to be joined by a large number of Mexicans who are disaffected with the government, as also a number that would or could be coerced into measures of subordination, they would soon possess themselves of Mexico. They would then attack the United States.

They said that the white men had now driven the Indian bands from the East to the West, and now they would work this plan to drive the whites out of the country; they said that the white people had got almost around them, and in a short time they would drive them again. I do believe that almost every band or nation of Indians was represented in that Council, and there was but one thing that was left unsettled, that was the time of attack—some said, the spring of 1838, and others said the spring of 1839; though this matter was to be left measurably to the Northern Indians, and to be communicated to the chiefs of the Comanches. The Council continued in session seven days, and at the end of that period, they broke up. One Indian came to me on the prairie, and stated that he was a Beadie, that he lived on the San Jacinto river, and that they were determined to make servants of the white people, and cursed me in the English language, which were the only English words I had heard during my captivity.

On one occasion, my young mistress and myself were out a short distance from town. She ordered me to go back to the town and get a kind of instrument with which they dig roots. Having lived as long, and indeed longer than life was desirable, I determined to aggravate them to kill me.

I told her I would not go back. She, in an enraged tone, bade me go. I told her I would not. She then with savage screams ran at me. I knocked, or, rather, pushed her down. She, fighting and screaming like a desperado, tried to get up; but I kept her down; and in the fight I got hold of a large buffalo bone. I beat her over the head with it, although expecting at every moment to feel a spear reach my heart from one of the Indians; but I lost no time. I was determined if they killed me, to make a cripple of her. Such yells as the Indians made around us—being nearly all collected—a Christian mind cannot conceive. No one touched me. I had her past hurting me, and indeed, nearly past breathing, when she cried out for mercy. I

108

let go my hold of her, and could but be amazed that not one of them attempted to arrest or kill me, or do the least thing for her. She was bleeding freely; for I had cut her head in several places to the skull. I raised her up and carried her to the camp.

A new adventure this. I was yet undetermined what would grow out of it. All the Indians seemed as unconcerned as if nothing had taken place. I washed her face and gave her water. She appeared remarkably friendly. One of the big chiefs came to me, and appeared to watch my movements with a great deal of attention. At length he observed—

"You are brave to fight—good to a fallen enemy—you are directed by the Great Spirit. Indians do not have pity on a fallen enemy. By our law you are clear. It is contrary to our law to show foul play. She began with you, and you had a right to kill her. Your noble spirit forbid you. When Indians fight, the conqueror gives or takes the life of his antagonist—and they seldom spare them."

This was like balm to my soul. But my old mistress was very mad. She ordered me to go and get a large bundle of straw. I soon learned it was to burn me to death. I did not fear that death; for I had prepared me a knife, with which I intended to defeat her object in putting me to death by burning, having determined to take my own life. She ordered me to cross my hands. I told her I would not do it. She asked me if I was willing for her to burn me to death without being tied. I told her that she should not tie me. She caught up a small bundle of the straw, and setting it on fire, threw it on me. I soon found I could not stand fire. I told her that I should fight if she burnt me any more, (she had already burnt me to blisters in many places.) An enraged tiger could not have screamed with more terrific violence than she did. She set another bundle on fire, and threw it on me. I was as good as my word. I pushed her into the fire, and as she raised, I knocked her down into the fire again, and kept her there until she was as badly burned as I was. She got hold of a club and hit me a time or two. I took it from her, and knocked her down with it. So we had a regular fight. I handled her with more ease than I did the young woman. During the fight, we had broken down one side of the house, and had got fully out into the street. After I had fully overcome her, I discovered the same diffidence on the part of the Indians as in the other fight. The whole of them were around us, screaming as before, and no one touched

109

us. I, as in the former case, immediately administered to her. All was silent again, except now and then, a grunt from the old woman. The young woman refused to help me into the house with her. I got her in, and then fixed up the side of the house that we had broken.

Next morning, twelve of the chiefs assembled at the Council House. We were called for, and we attended; and with all the solemnity of a church service, went into the trial. The old lady told the whole story without the least embellishment. I was asked if these things were so. I answered, "Yes." The young woman was asked, "Are these things true?" She said they were. We were asked if we had any thing to say. Both of the others said "No." I said I had. I told the Court that they had mistreated me—they had not taken me honorably; that they had used the white flag to deceive us, by which they had killed my friends—that I had been faithful, and had served them from fear of death, and that I would now rather die than be treated as I had been. I said that the Great Spirit would reward them for their treachery and their abuse to me. The sentence was, that I should get a new pole for the one that we had broken in the fight. I agreed to it, provided the young woman helped me. This was made a part of the decree, and all was peace again.

This answered me a valuable purpose afterwards, in some other instances. I took my own part, and fared much the better by it.

I shall next speak of the manners and customs of the Indians, and in this I shall be brief—as their habits are so ridiculous that this would be of but little interest to any.

They never stay more than three or four days in one place, unless it is in very cold weather; in that case, they stay until the weather changes. Their houses are made of skins, stretched on poles, which they always carry with them. Their poles are tied together, and put on each side of a mule, whilst one end drags on the ground. The women do all the work, except killing the meat. They herd the horses, saddle and pack them, build the houses, dress the skins, meat, &c. The men dance every night, during which, the women wait on them with water.

No woman is admitted into any of their Councils; nor is she allowed to enquire what their councils have been. When they move, the women do not know where they are going. They are no more than servants, and are looked upon and treated as such.

I knew one young man have his mother hung for refusing to get him feathers for his arrows, and appeared rejoiced at her death.

They are traditionary in their manner of cooking. It is considered a great sin, and sure defeat, to suffer meat to be broiled and boiled on the same fire at the same time. Every kind of provision has to be cooked and eaten by itself. When meat is broiling, or boiling, no person is allowed to pass so near as to suffer their shadow to pass over the meat, or it is not fit to eat. They often eat their meat entirely raw. When they kill meat, they suffer nothing to be lost. They have rigid laws, and rigorously enforce them when violated. They know no such thing as mercy. They have no language to express gratitude, only to say I am glad.

Dancing is a part of their worship. Torturing their prisoners is another. They pay their homage to a large lump of platina,* which lays in the Cross Timbers, on the waters of the Brazos. Every year, the chiefs collect sacrifices, and offer them to this their God. These offerings consist of beads, muscle shells, perriwinkles, &c. There are several bushels of beads that have been left there as sacrifices. They worship different things while on the prairie. Some worship a pet crow—some a deer skin, with the sun and moon pictured on it. The band that I was with, worshipped an eagle's wing. Those things are kept as sacredly by them, as the Holy Scriptures are by us. They drink water every morning until they vomit—particularly when they are going to war. They believe in a Supreme Being—the resurrection of the body, and in future rewards and punishments. I am informed, however, that some tribes do not believe in these things. These Indians are not countenanced by the others.

Their manner of doctoring by faith is amusing. When any of the men are sick, the principal civil chiefs order two of the wigwams to be joined together, though open between. A hole is dug in each of these camps, about two feet deep. In one of them, a fire is built; on the side of the other, is a lump of mud as large as a man's head. All around the hole, as well as this lump of mud, the ground is stuck full of willow sprouts. At sun-rise, the sick man and musicians enter the camps, and the music is kept up all day. No one must pass near enough to allow his shadow to fall on the camp, or the patient is sure to

---

* Platina is a scarce and valuable metal, heavier and more durable than gold. The Indians make arrow spikes of it sometimes. It is very malleable. This lump will weigh some thousands of pounds.

die; but if every thing is done right, he is sure to get well. If he dies, it is attributed to a failure in some of the ceremonies.

Having said as much on this subject as is necessary, I shall now return to my narrative.

On the head of Columbia river, I could sometimes get some dry brush to make me a light to work by. We were now in a very deep valley. One evening, I was going in search of some dry brush, and discovered some shining particles on the ground.

I picked up one of them. It was about three-fourths of an inch in circumference, of an oblong shape. I found it gave light, which superseded, ever afterward, the necessity of using dry brush. It was perfectly transparent. I leave my reader to judge what it was. I thought it was a diamond. There were unnumbered thousands of pieces. In some places, I could see the little ravine on which they were, at the distance of a mile, by the light which emanated from them. I lost this stone a few days before I was purchased. I have good reason to believe that one of the richest gold mines ever discovered may be found in that valley; and it would be a pity for so much wealth to remain undiscovered. The Indians often found pieces large enough to make arrow spikes, which is the only use they have for it. They would at any time exchange one of these arrow spikes for an iron one—the latter being harder and lighter. I may hereafter say more on this subject.

In the province or country called Senoro, I found many curiosities. (I, perhaps, may be mistaken as to the country; as all I know of it, I learned from the Indians and Mexican prisoners.) This country, I think, was a northwest course from Santa Fe, about 700 miles. Here I found a great curiosity in a kind of thorn, which is as complete a fish-hook as ever I saw, having several strong beards on each hook; and what is still more strange, there are various sizes on the same shrub. These hooks are quite as strong as any that are made of steel, and more elastic. I have two of them now that I have caught many a fish with. I took them off the bush myself, and have kept them ever since I have been released. I have often been offered five dollars for one of them, but I have never been induced to part with them. They often bring to my recollection the distant country where I obtained them.

In this region of country, nearly every shrub and tree bears a thorn or briar. The timber, what little there is, is very low and scrubby. I wish I had language to give a fair description of

112

this part of the country, with its present inhabitants. There are some Mexicans residing here. I tried to get one of them to buy me. I told him that even if my father and husband were dead, I knew I had land enough in Texas to fully indemnify him; but he did not try to buy me, although he agreed to do it. Some of the inhabitants are Indians. I am not certain of what tribe they are; but they cultivate the land, and raise some corn and potatoes. I was allowed to be among them but very little; neither do I believe them to be friendly with the Comanches— though I saw no quarrel between them; but the Comanches stole their horses and killed some of them as we were about leaving. I learned from the women that it was very seldom the Comanches went into that country. I saw here some springs that were truly a curiosity. The water, or kind of liquid, was about the consistency of tar, which would burn like oil, and was as yellow as gold. The earth, in many places, is also yellow. There are very few places in all this country, but what looks to be very poor. From the time that we left the country of the Rocky Mountains, and during the whole time we were in this region, I do not think I saw one tree more than fifteen feet high; and those, as before stated, covered with thorns. The healthiest looking Indians I ever saw, lived here. Notwithstanding it is a healthy country, I do not think it ever will be settled by white men, as I saw nothing to induce white men to settle there. I have neglected to mention that the Indians have very rigid laws in the collection of debts. If one man owes another, it stands perpetually as a debt until paid. When a creditor brings a suit for a debt, it is done by informing the civil chiefs. They immediately find out the amount due, which is recovered in buffalo skins, furs, mules, horses, bows, arrows, &c., according to the amount. The debtor is immediately informed of the amount that stands against him, and if he does not at once discharge the debt, it is in the power of the creditor, at any time, to enfore this judgment—which amounts to disfranchisement—that is, the debtor can hold no office, not even that of musician. He is not allowed to dance with his tribe, nor to hunt with them. If the debt is still unpaid when the debtor dies, his children are held under the same restrictions as those incurred by the father; nor are their wives allowed to associate with other women.

There are among them delinquent debtors, who are doubtless now bound for debts contracted by their forefathers five hundred years ago. Some use great exertions to pay the debt; but the last cent must be paid.

They have their different grades of officers, both civil and military. In many cases, these offices are hereditary. They enforce their laws most rigorously, even among themselves. They are strangers to any thing like mercy or sympathy, unless it is in war. They appear to be much enraged at the death of one of their men—particularly if their dead are scalped. If their dead are not scalped, they do not mind it so much. When they have a battle, every exertion to prevent their dead from falling into the hands of the enemy is made, even to the extent of risking their own lives, which they often lose in trying to save, or carry off their dead from the field of battle. If they cannot get the body, they take off the scalp or head of their slain—such is their aversion to the enemy becoming possessed of the scalp The scalps of their enemies are kept as securities of good luck. This good luck is transferable from the father to the son.

On one occasion, they had a very severe battle with the Osage Indians, in which the Comanches lost several men. Part of them fell into the hands of the Osages. They secured the heads of some, and from others they took their scalps; yet the Osages got some of them. They grived much more for those who had been scalped, than for those that were not.

In this battle, the Comanches got hold of several of the Osages that were killed, and brought their bodies to the town. They cut them up, broiled and boiled and ate them. My young mistress got a foot, roasted it, and offered me part of it. They appear to be very fond of human flesh. The hand or foot, they say, is the most delicious.

These inhuman cannibals will eat the flesh of a human being and talk of their bravery or abuse their cowardice with as much unconcern as if they were mere beasts.

One evening as I was at my work, (being north of the Rocky Mountains,) I discovered some Mexican traders.* Hope instantly mounted the throne from whence it had long been banished. My tottering frame received fresh life and courage, as I saw them approaching the habitation of sorrow and grief where I dwelt. They asked for my master, and we were directly with

---

* I had dreamed, the night before, that I saw an angel, the same I saw in the cave. He had four wings. He gave them to me, and immediately I was on the wing, and was soon with my father. But, when I awoke, behold! it was all a dream.

him. They asked if he would sell me. No music, no sounds that ever reached my anxious ear, was half so sweet as *"ce senure,"* (yes, sir.) The trader made an offer for me. My owner refused. He offered more, but my owner still refused. Utter confusion hovers around my mind while I record this part of my history; and I can only ask my reader, if he can, to fancy himself in my situation; for language will fail to describe the anxious thoughts that revolved in my throbbing breast when I heard the trader say he could give no more. Oh! had I the treasures of the universe, how freely I would have given it; yea, and then consented to have been a servant to my countrymen. Would that my father could speak to him; but my father is no more. Or one of my dear uncles; yes, they would say "stop not for price." Oh! my good Lord, intercede for me. My eyes, despite my efforts, are swimming in tears at the very thought. I only have to appeal to the treasure of your hearts, my readers, to conceive the state of my desponding mind at this crisis. At length, however, the trader made another offer for me, which my owner agreed to take. My whole feeble frame was now convulsed in an ecstasy of joy, as he delivered the first article as an earnest of the trade. MEMORABLE DAY!

Col. Nathaniel Parker, of Charleston, Illinois, burst into my mind; and although I knew he was about that time in the Illinois Senate, I knew he would soon reach his suffering niece, if he could only hear of her. Yes, I knew he would hasten to my relief, even at the sacrifice of a seat in that honorable body, if necessary.

Thousands of thoughts revolved through my mind as the trader was paying for me. My joy was full. Oh! shall I ever forget the time when my new master told me to go with him to his tent? As I turned from my prison, in my very soul I tried to return thanks to my God who always hears the cries of his saints:

My God was with me in distress,
My God was always there;
Oh! may I to my God address
Thankful and devoted prayer.

I was soon informed by my new master that he was going to take me to Santa Fe. That night, sleep departed from my eyes. In my fancy I surveyed the steps of my childhood, in company with my dear relations. It would, I suppose, be needless for me to say that I watched with eagerness the day to spring, and that the night was long filled with gratitude to the Divine Conservator of the divine law of heaven and earth.

In the morning quite early, all things being ready, we started. We traveled very hard for seventeen days, when we reached Santa Fe. Then, my reader, I beheld some of my countrymen, and I leave you to conjecture the contrast in my feelings when I found myself surrounded by sympathising Americans, clad in decent attire. I was soon conducted to Col. William Donoho's residence. I found that it was him who had heard of the situation of myself and others, and being an American indeed, his manly and magnanimous bosom, heaved with sympathy characteristic of a Christian, had devised the plan for our release.* Here I was at home. I hope that every American that reads this narrative may duly appreciate this amiable man, to whom, under the providence of God, I owe my release. I have no language to express my gratitude to Mrs. Donoho. I found in her a mother, to direct me in that strange land, a sister to condole with me in my misfortune, and offer new scenes of amusement to me to revive my mind. A friend? yes, the best of friends; one who had been blessed with plenty, and was anxious to make me comfortable; and one who was continually pouring the sweet oil of consolation into my wounded and trembling soul, and was always comforting and admonishing me not to despond, and assured me that every thing should be done to facilitate my return to my relatives; and though I am now separated far from her, I still owe to her a debt of gratitude I shall never be able to repay but with my earnest prayers for the blessing of God to attend her through life.

The people of Santa Fe, by subscription, made up $150 to assist me to my friends. This was put into the hands of Rev. C*********,† who kept it and never let me have it; and but for the kindness of Mr. and Mrs. Donoho, I could not have got along. Soon after I arrived in Santa Fe, a disturbance took place among the Mexicans. They killed several of their leading men. Mr. Donoho considered it unsafe for his family, and started with them to Missouri, and made me welcome as one of his family. The road led through a vast region of prairie, which is nearly one thousand miles across. This, to many, would have been a considerable undertaking, as it was all the way through

---

* Mrs. Harris had also been purchased by his arrangements.
† At the request of my father I forbear publishing his name.

116

an Indian country. But we arrived safely at Independence, in Missouri, where I received many signal favors from many of the inhabitants, for which I shall ever feel grateful. I stayed at Mr. Donoho's but I was impatient to learn something of my relatives.

My anxiety grew so great that I was often tempted to start on foot. I tried to pray, mingling my tears and prayers to Almighty God to intercede for me, and in his providence to devise some means by which I might get home to my friends. Despite of all the kind entreaties of that benevolent woman, Mrs. Donoho, I refused to be comforted; and who, I ask, under these circumstances, could have been reconciled?

One evening I had been in my room trying to pray, and on stepping to the door, I saw my brother-in-law, Mr. Nixon. I tried to run to him, but was not able. I was so much overjoyed I scarcely knew what to say or how to act. I asked, "are my father and husband alive?" He answered affirmatively. "Are mother and the children alive?" He said they were. Every moment seemed an hour. It was very cold weather, being now in dead of winter.

Mr. Donoho furnished me a horse, and in a few days we started, Mr. Donoho accompanying us. We had a long and cold journey of more than one thousand miles, the way we were compelled to travel, and that principally through a frontier country. But having been accustomed to hardships, together with my great anxiety, I thought I could stand any thing, and the nearer I approached my people, the greater my anxiety grew. Finally on the evening of the 19th day of February, 1838, I arrived at my father's house in Montgomery county, Texas. Here united tears of joy flowed from the eyes of father, mother, brothers and sisters; while many strangers, unknown to me, (neighbors to my father) cordially united in this joyful interview.

I am now not only freed from my Indian captivity, enjoying the exquisite pleasure that my soul has long panted for.

> Oh! God of Love, with pitying eye
> Look on a wretch like me;
> That I may on thy name rely,
> Oh, Lord! be pleased to see.
>
> How oft have sighs unuttered flowed
> From my poor wounded heart,
> Yet thou my wishes did reward,
> And sooth'd the painful smart.

117

The following lines were written by Mrs. Plummer just before her death. Although they will not bear a critic's eye, yet we have thought we would append them to her narrative.

Ye careless ones, who wildly stroll
On life's uneven tide—
List to the sorrows of my soul,
My heaving bosom hide.

Oh, parents will you lend an ear,
And listen to my grief;
Will you let fall for me one tear,
Or could this give relief?

But, oh, my soul! my darling babe,
Was from my bosom torn,
It lies now in deaths gloomy shade,
And I am left to mourn.

Good LORD, I cried can I endure,
Such sorrow and deep grief,
His holy spirit kind and pure,
Give my poor soul relief.

It is very much to be regreted, that this little history of the capture of the Parker Fort by the Indians, and the trials and suffering the survivors had to endure, was not kept intact, we feel it our duty to republish all that is left intelligible of this little book, every effort to obain a full copy having failed.

James W. Parker narrator

John Parker Elder of
Baptist Church — father
of James W. Parker and
Daniel Parker (ancestor of the Audie(?)
Co. Parkers) d. 1844 buried Elkhart Texas

Benjamin killed by
Indians May 19. 1836
Silas — father of Cynthia
Ann + John —

Nathaniel remained
in Illinois

Cynthia Ann +
children of Silas and
by Indians May 19. 1836
John found his way back
his mother uncle

James S. Parker
wounded and recovered

Rachel Plummer +
Mrs. Nixon daughter
of James W. Parker

James Pratt Plummer
taken from mother by
Indians — later

Mrs. Clemmer & Son captured
by Indians May 19, 1836

Samuel Frost   killed May
Robert Frost, son of Samuel
G. E. Dwight   son-in-law
of Samuel Frost